First World War
and Army of Occupation
War Diary
France, Belgium and Germany

57 DIVISION
Divisional Troops
Machine Gun Corps
57 Battalion
15 June 1916 - 26 May 1919

WO95/2974/4

The Naval & Military Press Ltd
www.nmarchive.com
Published in association with The National Archives

Published by

The Naval & Military Press Ltd

Unit 10 Ridgewood Industrial Park,

Uckfield, East Sussex,

TN22 5QE England

Tel: +44 (0) 1825 749494

www.naval-military-press.com

www.nmarchive.com

This diary has been reprinted in facsimile from the original. Any imperfections are inevitably reproduced and the quality may fall short of modern type and cartographic standards.

© **Crown Copyright**
Images reproduced by permission of The National Archives, London, England, 2015.

Contents

Document type	Place/Title	Date From	Date To
Heading	WO95/2974-4		
Heading	57 Bn Machine Gun Corps 1918 Mar-1919 Mar		
Heading	57th Battalion Machine Gun Corps April 1918		
War Diary	Map Lens II	01/04/1918	01/04/1918
War Diary	Map Sheet 51c V.2c.2.9		
War Diary	Map Lens II		
War Diary	Map Sheet 57D 1.40000		
War Diary	Map Sheet 57 D NE 1/20,000 Coigneux	01/05/1918	08/05/1918
War Diary	Couin Coigneux Gommecourt Hebuterne	08/05/1918	08/05/1918
War Diary	Map Sheet 57 D NE 1/20,000	12/05/1918	12/05/1918
War Diary	Couin Coigneux Gommecourt He Bethune	12/05/1918	25/05/1918
War Diary	Map Sheet 57 D N E 1/20,000	25/05/1918	01/06/1918
War Diary	Couin Hebuterne Gommecourt Coigneux	02/06/1918	13/06/1918
War Diary	Map Sheet 57 D N E 1/20,000	15/06/1916	25/06/1916
War Diary	Lens II 1/40,000 Bois De Warnimont Couin Bois De Warnimont Bus Orville	01/07/1918	01/07/1918
War Diary	Lens II 1/40,000 Bois De Warnimont	18/07/1918	21/07/1918
War Diary	Beaudricourt	29/07/1918	29/07/1918
War Diary	Gouves	31/07/1918	31/07/1918
War Diary	Lens Map 1/40,000 Duisans Arras	01/08/1918	22/08/1918
War Diary	Sombrin	23/08/1918	23/08/1918
War Diary	Ref Map Sheet 51 B N W U 1/10,000 Lens 1/10.0000	18/08/1918	20/08/1918
War Diary	Sombrin Bavincourt Bretencourt Ransart	25/08/1918	25/08/1918
War Diary	Blaireville	26/08/1918	26/08/1918
War Diary	Mercatel		
War Diary	Reference Lens II Sheet 51 B.S.W 1/20,000	27/08/1918	27/08/1918
War Diary	Blaireville Henin Mercatel Fontaine	28/08/1918	28/08/1918
War Diary	Ref Lens II 1/10,000 Sheet 50 B Mercatel Henin Fontaine Hendecourt	28/08/1918	31/08/1918
Miscellaneous	57th Battn. N.C.C. Operation Order No. 25 App A	27/08/1918	27/08/1918
Heading	57 Bn M.G. Corps Vol 8 Sep 1918		
Miscellaneous	On His Majesty's Service.		
Miscellaneous	D A G 3rd Echelon	27/10/1918	27/10/1918
Miscellaneous	H.Q. 57th Division (G)		
War Diary	Ref Sheet 51 B S Q 1/20,000 Henin Hill Fontaine Hendecourt Riencourt	01/09/1918	01/09/1918
War Diary	Ref Map 57 D SW L 51 D SE 1/20,000 Hendecourt Riencourt	02/09/1918	02/09/1918
War Diary	51b S W & SE 1/20,000 57 C NE 1/20000 Hendecourt Lez Cagnicourt	03/09/1918	03/09/1918
War Diary	Inchy-En-Artois Sector	08/09/1918	09/09/1918
War Diary	Sheet 57 N NE 1/20000		
War Diary	Moeuvres	09/09/1918	11/09/1918
War Diary	Sheet 57 M 1/20000	12/09/1918	17/09/1918
War Diary	Map Ref. Lens II 1/100,000 57c. 1/40,000 57c N.E. 1/20,000 Monchiet	17/09/1918	26/09/1918
War Diary	Monchiet	20/09/1918	24/09/1918
War Diary	Noreuil	25/09/1918	27/09/1918
War Diary	Pronville	27/09/1918	27/09/1918

War Diary	Map. Ref. 57c N.E. 1/20,000 57b N.W. Pronville Moeuvres Anneux Cantaing Fontaine Notre Dame Proville	27/09/1918	30/09/1918
Miscellaneous			
Operation(al) Order(s)	57th Battn. M.G.C. Operation Order No. 26 App A (1)	31/08/1918	31/08/1918
Miscellaneous	57th Battn. M.G.C. Warning Order App A	31/08/1918	31/08/1918
Miscellaneous	Warning Order App B	01/08/1918	01/08/1918
Miscellaneous	57th Battn. M.G.C. Operation Order App C	02/09/1918	02/09/1918
Miscellaneous	57th Battn. M.G.C. Operation Order No. 26 App D	11/09/1918	11/09/1918
Miscellaneous	57th Battn. M.G.C. Operation Order No. 30 App E	14/09/1918	14/09/1918
Miscellaneous	Reference 57th Battn M. G. Operation Order No 30 Para 5	15/09/1918	15/09/1918
Miscellaneous	57th Bn M.G.C. Operation Order No. 31	16/09/1918	16/09/1918
Miscellaneous	57th Battn M.G.C. Warning Order App G.	23/09/1918	23/09/1918
Miscellaneous	57th Battn. M.G.C. Operation Order No. 32 App H	24/09/1918	24/09/1918
Miscellaneous	57th Battn. M.G.C. Instruction No. 1 App J	23/09/1918	23/09/1918
Miscellaneous	Account Of 57th Battn. M.G.C. Operation App K		
Miscellaneous	H Q 57th Divn (G)	07/11/1918	07/11/1918
War Diary		01/10/1918	13/10/1918
War Diary	Map Sheet 57c 44b Bethune Central 36		
War Diary	Moeuvres	10/10/1918	12/10/1918
War Diary	Fouquereuil Braquemont	13/10/1918	13/10/1918
War Diary	Pont Riqueul Bout Deville Fromelles	14/10/1916	14/10/1916
War Diary	Pont Riqueul Fromelles	15/10/1918	15/10/1918
War Diary	Pont Riqueul	16/10/1918	16/10/1918
War Diary	Fromelles	17/10/1918	17/10/1918
War Diary	Sheet 36 & 37 Englos	18/10/1918	18/10/1918
War Diary	Pt Ronchin (Lille)	19/10/1918	20/10/1918
War Diary	Willems (Le Daru)	21/10/1918	21/10/1918
War Diary	Sheet 37 Le Daru	22/10/1918	29/10/1918
War Diary	Sheet 36 Mons En Baroeul	30/10/1918	31/10/1918
Miscellaneous	57th Battn. M.G.C. Account Of Operation App I	09/10/1918	09/10/1918
Miscellaneous	Remarks		
Miscellaneous	57th Battn. M.G.C. Warning Order App II	13/10/1918	13/10/1918
Miscellaneous	57th Battn. M.G.C. Operation Order No. 41 App III	14/10/1918	14/10/1918
Miscellaneous	57th Battn. M.G.C. App IV	16/10/1918	16/10/1918
Miscellaneous	57th Battn. M.G.C. Operation Order No. 42 App V	24/10/1918	24/10/1918
Miscellaneous	57th Battn. M.G.C. Instruction For The Defence App Vi	29/10/1918	29/10/1918
Miscellaneous	57th Battn. M.G.C. App VIII	29/10/1918	29/10/1918
War Diary		01/11/1918	30/11/1918
War Diary	Sheet 36 & 5 Mons On Baroeul (Lille)	01/12/1918	03/12/1918
War Diary	Carvin Gouves & Contenescourt	04/12/1918	21/12/1918
War Diary	Ouves	22/12/1918	31/12/1918
War Diary	Sheet 57c Gouves Montenescourt	02/01/1919	03/01/1919
War Diary	Habarcq Sheet 51c	05/01/1919	12/01/1919
War Diary	Robecq	13/01/1919	31/01/1919
War Diary	Habarcq Chateau Sheet 51c	02/02/1919	28/02/1919
War Diary	Robecq Chateau Ref 1/18 Maroeuil 19-31 Sheet 51c	01/03/1919	28/03/1919
War Diary	57th Battn. Machine Gun Corps Operation Order No. 46	13/03/1919	13/03/1919
War Diary	Maroeuil Sheet 51c France	01/04/1919	26/05/1919

ಜಗ/2974(4)

ಜಗ/2974(4)

57 DIV TROOPS

57 BN MACHINE GUN CORPS

1918 MAR — 1919 MAY

57th Divisional M.G.C.

WAR DIARY

57th BATTALION

MACHINE GUN CORPS

APRIL 1918

57 Bn M.G.C. Army Form C. 2118.

WAR DIARY
INTELLIGENCE SUMMARY.
(Erase heading not required.)

Instructions regarding War Diaries and Intelligence Summaries are contained in F.S. Regs., Part II. and the Staff Manual respectively. Title pages will be prepared in manuscript.

Place	Date	Hour	Summary of Events and Information	Remarks and references to Appendices
Maps: Sheet II	April 1st		The Batt. were relieved by the 40th Bn. M.G.C. as under:—	
			B Coy. 40th Bn. relieved C Coy. 57th Bn. ⎫ on the night of 31st March/1st April	
			D Coy. " " D Coy. " " ⎬	
			E Coy. " " B Coy. " " ⎭	
			A Coy. " " A Coy. " " on the night of the 1st/2nd April.	
			The relief was carried out with two casualties, one killed 81057055 Pte. HUDSON A. C Coy. and one wounded 201402362 Pte. LAWTON L.D. by intruded, who remained at duty.	
			C Coy. marched to billets in ESTAIRES and thence to HAVERSKERQUE. D Coy. to NOUVEAU MONDE and thence to Gare de la ville MERVILLE. B Coy. to ESTAIRES and A Coy. remained at SAILLY. H.Q. moved to MERVILLE on completion of the relief.	
			The Battalion moved to MONDICOURT by train as follows:— On April 2nd A Coy from CALONNE. B Coy from MERVILLE, C Coy from STEENBECQUE. On April 3rd H.Q. & D Coy from CALONNE.	
			Billets were allotted as under in this area.	
			B/HQ. LUCHEUX. 46.95.B5	
			A. Coy. " 45.85.88	
			B. Coy. GROUCHES 45 59.16	
			C. Coy. " 45 6.2	
			D. Coy. LUCHEUX B.4	

Lt Col
Comdg. 57th Bn. M.G.C.
1/5/18

Army Form C. 2118.

WAR DIARY
OF
INTELLIGENCE SUMMARY.
(Erase heading not required.)

Instructions regarding War Diaries and Intelligence Summaries are contained in F. S. Regs., Part II. and the Staff Manual respectively. Title pages will be prepared in manuscript.

Place	Date	Hour	Summary of Events and Information	Remarks and references to Appendices
MAP. LENS II.			The Battalion now joined the VI Corps on the 3rd Army. The Battalion was still in Reserve Army front of the VI Corps front. The VI Corps was under the command of Lt.Gen. Sir AYLMER HALDANE K.C.B. D.S.O. and the 3rd Army under Sir JULIAN BYNG. K.C.B. K.C.M.G. M.V.O	
Map. Sheet 51.c V.2 & 2.9.			On April 4th the Batt. moved by train to SAULTY, at an hour's notice. H.Q. were at V.2 & 2.9. the men were in billets and all the officers in the Y.M.C.A. hut. On April 5th the Batt. was placed on 1 hours notice to move from 8 a.m. to 12 noon and at 2 hours notice for the rest of the 24 hours daily. Training continued was carried on in the mornings.	
Map. LENS II.			On April 7th the Batt. moved to BEAUQUESNE by road. H.Qrs. were located at 5.E.27.5.13. The whole Batt. being billeted in the town. The Battalion still remained in the 3rd Army Reserve but in hour admiration held by the VI Corps commanded by Lt.Gen. Sir G.M. HARPER. K.C.B. D.S.O. A reconnaissance of the RED LINE was carried out by officers. On April 12th the Batt. marched to LUCHEUX via ORVILLE & HALLOY and occupied the same billets as before except that B Coy. & Coy. were billeted in LUCHEUX instead of GROUCHES.	
Map. Sheet 57 D.1.40.m			On April 13th the Batt. marched to AUTHY and camped in the huts S.E. of the village.	

WAR DIARY

INTELLIGENCE SUMMARY.

(Erase heading not required.)

Army Form C. 2118.

Place	Date	Hour	Summary of Events and Information	Remarks and references to Appendices
M.A.P. Sht 57 D 19 n.w.			On April 16th the Battn. marched to COIGNEUX and encamped in huts and tents at J 9 c. 0.5.	
			On April 18th D Coy moved on detachment to HENU and camped at D 19 a. 3. 3.	
			The reconnoitring of the RED LINE and CHATEAU DE LA HAIE switch was carried on.	
			Arrangements were also made to hold the PURPLE and RED systems as under:	
			A Coy and 170 Bde CHATEAU de LA HAIE switch, B & C Coys with 171 & 172 Bdes holding RED LINE from J 11 central to E 13 central. Div. HQn in Battle & D Coy at HENU.	
			Position here dug & ammunition reserve arranged.	
			On the 20th Capt T.N.F. WILSON M.C. 1st B. 60 Rifles joined the Battalion and assumed the duties of Adjutant – Under some difficulties owing to lack of a working knowledge of French. An Horses etc. commenced on the 21st. The personnel of H.Q. Staff on transfer for the Adjutant near days have but only improved slightly.	
			On the 23rd Major J.A. BARRACLOUGH M.C. returned from the American Army school and resumed command of A Coy – about 8.45 p.m. the Camp was slightly shelled by H.E. and the Batt: lost 1 O.R. killed staterns – There were only 3 slight casualties.	No. 58723 Pte DIXON H. " 205511 " HASLOW S. of letter " 22637 " MERCER J. of letter

[signature] 15/5/18

WAR DIARY
or
INTELLIGENCE SUMMARY
(Erase heading not required.)

Army Form C. 2118.

Place	Date	Hour	Summary of Events and Information	Remarks and references to Appendices
			Two sections of A Coy were sent to man trenches in rear of CHATEAU DE LA HAIE should Germans — At 2.45ᵃᵐ the C.O commenced an inspection of the Battalion beginning to Coy (B sector) and B Coy on their Hdqts and D Coy on HQ 26 Point. Two French survivors of the 129ᵗʰ & 141ˢᵗ arrived in the area in the 18ᵗʰ Point, but the expected attack not developing they left to the NORTH in HQ 28 F x 30 F. It was decided to call the Rear Battalion to include the BAYENCOURT Station forming the PURPLE LINE at the CHATEAU de la HAIE Coy and Bⁿ HQrs were constructed and the necessary improvements made to the defences. The main phase improvements were as follows — On the 30ᵗʰ the new "Battle Positions" were given and Coys took up their positions in the RED and PURPLE Lines. Coys were in British trenches and below and thirty mounted upts were being dug.	1/5/18 1/5/18 Comdg 5ᵗʰ Bn 14.c

WAR DIARY
or
INTELLIGENCE SUMMARY
(Erase heading not required.)

Army Form C. 2118.

57 Bn. M.G. Corps   Vol 4

Place	Date	Hour	Summary of Events and Information	Remarks and references to Appendices
VLAM: ERTINGHE C.57 DNE 1/20,000 COLMEUR	1/3/18		For the first week of May the Battalion was still in Army Reserve. A Coy (Newfield) B & C Coys and Bn HQ in camp at TQC. D Coy at MENY and two sections of A Coy in the Nth line in front of CHATEAU DE LA HAIE and Bully en Bois. Bn in Nth line were continued with 37.74 [?] 7th Division 3rd Army who reported that for seven to ten days or so good work at LANGEMARCK in November 1917. The Division had been warned that they could relieve the 42nd Division in the Nieuport Sector 17-18th June in the near future. The gun teams were carried out.	
	5/5/18		The Coys commenced on the night of the 5/6th May machine gun relays taking place 24 hrs after it.	
	6/5/18		Supplies, Ammunition etc. & rations were sent into the line & the Coys before the relief. D and C Coys relieved on the night of the 6/7/18 (?) by ____ (?) sent into the left sects of the Nieuport front. D Coy sent into support.	
	7/5/18		Major G.L. Wade MC was transferred for duty as second in command to the 48th Bn. M.G.C. Capt S.H.B Livingstone commanded Bn. Burning of the 7th May A Coy moved into Nieuport front on the night 7/8th May sent to the left sector of the divisional front.	
	8/5/18		Bn transferred. On the morning of the 8th May the Bn HQ moved to COUIN. Concentration of which the Bn was located is under:	

Bn H.Q.   COUIN   TUBES
B   ""   Rossignol
A Coy HQ   COLINCOX   Indian
B   ""   COMMECOURT E29a3.3
C   ""   ""   E29.13.9
D   ""   HEBUTERNE N3c4.4

The relief was carried out without any casualties but there were 50 on the L.C.

COUIN
BOUCOIN
COMMECOURT
HEBUTERNE

WAR DIARY
or
INTELLIGENCE SUMMARY.

(Erase heading not required.)

Army Form C. 2118.

Instructions regarding War Diaries and Intelligence
Summaries are contained in F. S. Regs., Part II.
and the Staff Manual respectively. Title pages
will be prepared in manuscript.

Place	Date	Hour	Summary of Events and Information	Remarks and references to Appendices
Map Sheet 7 D N E 1/20,000			The trenches when taken over were in a bad condition and much work had to be done. New gun positions were made and those existing improved. The enemy were not active and except for the occasional shelling of selected targets which was not interfered with.	
FOUIX COUNEUX BONNECOURT HEROSCANE	12/5/18		On the night of the 12th FONQUEVILLERS was bombarded with yellow cross gas shells. The village had to be cleared and a section of D Coy immediately south of the village who were in the area bombarded had to evacuate their positions temporarily. ~~during~~ the gas hung about for some hours after the bombardment & this section had 18 gas casualties. One man was killed by the first shell that fell. Both the 37th Division & the 37th Division suffered considerably from this bombardment. Some 20,000 shells were said to have fallen in the vicinity.	See Appendix A
	13/5/18		On the night 13/14th A Coy relieved B Coy in the left sector. While the relief was in progress the enemy started to shell the road on which the horses were. A Coy lost 4 wounded and 2 killed. B Coy 3 killed. Four mules and a riding horse were also killed.	See Appendix A
	16/5/18		On the night 16/17th the Battalion carried out a harassing shoot on selected targets. This must have annoyed the enemy as there was some retaliation. 22 guns employed searching in enfiladments by lists.	
	21/5/18		On the night of the 21/22nd B Coy relieved C Coy in the right section of the divisional front.	
	22/5/18		On the night of the 21st/22nd the 2/4th S. Lancs Regt carried out a raid on the enemys trenches in R.H.C. The raiding party consisted of one Company supported by Artillery and machine guns. Three prisoners were captured four of whom did not reach our lines having given some trouble. 22 m.g. supported the Raid with barrage fire which was not successful in preventing enemys ~~movement~~ saving casualties. There were 12 only wounded & of these remained at duty.	

A 5834 Wt. W4973 M687 750,000 8/16 D. D. & L. Ltd. Forms/C.2118/13.

WAR DIARY
or
INTELLIGENCE SUMMARY.

Army Form C. 2118.

(Erase heading not required.)

Place	Date	Hour	Summary of Events and Information	Remarks and references to Appendices
Trench Sheet 57 S NE 1/20,000	28/9/17		During the 25th and 26th enemy artillery seemed to attach importance to a barrage on the evening of the 27th. Apparently the rumoured artillery attack was in conjunction with the attack	
			Other MINES and TORPEDOS. On the 22nd of the month LIEUT WM PROPER joined the Battalion.	
	29/9/17		On the night of the 29/30th C & Q wished D Coy in support. During the 27th & 28th 3 guns & what I believe were rifle grenades were thrown at sentries connecting to the Batterie without causing much damage. The enemy has [rejected] talk peace with no [-------] to that end by the Generally throughout the sector he [said] was no [-----] when he retreated when he was patching in nature. He has was a very quiet and until 1130 [---] were firing practically [---] + shelling in nature.	
	30/9/17	11.30 a.m	heavy shell burst out 16 guns in ROOM trenches about 25th of [------] found.	

Army Form C. 2118.

WAR DIARY
or
INTELLIGENCE SUMMARY.
(Erase heading not required.)

Appendix A.

Place	Date	Hour	Summary of Events and Information	Remarks and references to Appendices

Instructions regarding War Diaries and Intelligence Summaries are contained in F.S. Regs., Part II. and the Staff Manual respectively. Title pages will be prepared in manuscript.

Casualties

Killed in Action

			Place of Burial
57322	Pte Hambridge, G.	11.5.18	Goulin Cemetry J.r.b.65.9.3
60613	L/C Morrison, R.	14.5.18	do
39506	Pte Read, W.	"	do
128127	" Spencer, A.	"	do
127980	" Goldthorpe, G.F.	"	do
67201	" Hunt, J.	25.5.18	do

Died of Wounds

| 128387 | Pte Bernard, W. | 14.5.18 | do |
| 122166 | L/C Watson, N. | 19.5.18 | do |

Wounded -(Shell fire, etc)

140329	Pte Brookes, R.R.	8.5.18
140322	" Christian, R.	9.5.18
58934	Cpl Densley, H.	10.5.18
140309	Pte Barnes, C.	13.5.18
36547	Cpl Crotl, J.	14.5.18
129191	Pte Brayshaw G.A.	"
70767	" Brown, M.	"
140316	" Evans, J.H.	"
119390	" Kegan, P.	22.5.18
141184	" Kendal, J.	"
128857	" Webster, J.	"
57095	Cpl Knight, J.C.	25.5.18
127727	Pte Pryer, F.E.	26.5.18
125166	" Smith, G.R.	27.5.18
138635	" Jeffrey, J.	29.5.18

Wounded Gas

5905	C.Q.M.S. Durrad, L.J.
62925	Cpl. Rowlands, W.
3585	" Moore, G.H.
32054	L/C Hampson, G.H.
140291	" Hill, J.
86629	Pte Hunt, W.J.
87531	" Robertson, J.
122655	" Gardner, W.J.
58062	" Richards, G.W.
13490	" Seamens, J.J.
103999	" Toffey, E.J.
27277	" Guthrie, Q.
103236	" Keath, L.H.
103161	" Preston, S.
34657	" Harris, A.J.
102475	" Shaw, D.
122928	" Edge, C.
65919	" Shuttleworth, W.
104993	L/C Hall, J.
45013	Pte Mitchell, R.R.
57060	" Gayton, B.
140226	" Heys, E.
3/238	C.Q.M.S. Crouch, C.
14635	L/C Brick, A.
123213	Pte Carter, G.
116265	" Kirkby, F.Q.
140342	" Smith, E.
140132	" Tunstall, A.

} 12.5.18

Total Casualties   3 K. 15 W. 28 G.

Army Form C. 2118.

57 Bn MG Corps
Vol 5

WAR DIARY
or
INTELLIGENCE SUMMARY.
(Erase heading not required)

Place	Date	Hour	Summary of Events and Information	Remarks and references to Appendices
High Wood - 57 DNE 1/20000	1/6/18		On the morning of the 1st June an enemy raiding party of 60 attempted to enter our lines East of HEBUTERNE. They were driven off leaving one wounded prisoner and other wounded and dead in front of our line. An S.O.S. was sent up during the raid and the Battalion fired 34,000 rounds so they were unable to see exactly what was happening. Lt. M.C. VYVYAN was wounded by a shell.	
COUIN HEBUTERNE GOMMECOURT COIGNEUX	2/3rd		On the night 2/3rd June the 114th L.M.M. were supposed to carry out a raid on the enemy's trenches in L.7.c. The greater part of the raiding party did not arrive at their assembly positions, and the raid was postponed at the last minute. This information did not reach the Battalion in time to stop the barrage. 34 guns from A,B,C Coys fired 53,500 rounds in support of the raid. The same operations were carried out the following night but did not meet with any success. Again the 34 guns from A,B,C Coys fired 54,000 rounds in support of the raid.	
	3rd/4th		Lt. PE CARA was struck off the strength of the Bn. having been invalided sick to England. 14730 Pte Snidyer was wounded by a shell 4/6/18.	
	8/6/18		On the evening of the 8th from 10.30 p.m. to 11 p.m. an incendiary shoot was carried out on REIGNON WOOD 4 guns from B and 10 from D co-operated with the R.A. 38,750 rounds were fired. The wood was not affected it is a thousand so fire was carried.	
	8th/9th		On the night 8/9th D Coy relieved A Coy in left section of Batt front. A Coy went into reserve at S.2.c.	
	11/6/18		On the 11th the section of the 2nd MG Grande were attached to the Bn. for instruction. One subsection sent to C Coy one to B and one section to D.	
	13/6/18		On the 13th Lieutn T.D. WARREN and Lieut. T.D. BROSTER proceeded to M.G. Training Centre GRANTHAM for a tour of duty at home. Lieut. D.C. DAVIS M.C. assumed the duties of 2nd in command A Coy.	

WAR DIARY
or
INTELLIGENCE SUMMARY
(Erase heading not required.)

Army Form C. 2118.

Place	Date	Hour	Summary of Events and Information	Remarks and references to Appendices
Hqts Bhd 57 D.N.E. 4/25,000	15/1/18		On the night 15/1/18 19 grenades from C.D., D, bays fired 16,100 rounds harassing fire—	
	16/1/17		On the night 16/1/17 C Coy more relieved of the 2nd Life Guards relieved the ahead in the line.	
			The same night A Coy relieved D Coy in the right section of the Battn front. B Coy went into Battn reserve at J.32.c.	
			1366 Sgt Seymour H.S. was wounded by a shell 17/1/18 and Lt. M.A. GARDNER was also slightly wounded but remained at duty.	
			26328 Sgt Merriman J.D. was mentioned in Despatches. London Gazette dated 4 Jan 1918.	
	18/1/18		On the 18.2 the area north of COMMECOURT was heavily shelled but P and S.Q. Lost enemy and damage was done except to the trenches.	
	19/1/18		On the 19th Lieut. B.W. DAVIES proceeded to M.G. Training Centre GRANTHAM for a term of duty at home.	
	20/21st		On the night of the 20/21st one by of the 2nd (Bn?) Dn. The King's (Liverpool Regt) carried out a raid on the enemy's trenches in K.11. c.d. Twelve guns from A by, eight from C and eight from D cooperated. 57 S.O.S. rounds were fired. One prisoner and one M.C. were captured.	
	21/1/18		On the 21st two more sections of the 2nd Life Guards arrived during to relieve of the 62nd Division as per A.D.S. which were later postponed. These two sections did not go into the line. None ahead in the line came out.	
			The following officers joined the Battalion 21/1/18 and were posted to bys as shown	Lieut. T.S. CLAY posted to 7 by F.C. PRICE — D " W. CLARK — C " H. REED — A
	24/25th 25th		86 Bdye McROY Z135.A was wounded by a shell 21/1/18. On the night 24/25 1/18 the 1/7th Sherwood Foresters 2nd Life Guards for the Battn — no relief Coy went into Night Reserve at J.32.c. On the night 25 the attached 2nd Life Guards for the Battn — part of a bye against the Life Guards having been transferred to another Bn.	

[signature] J.W. Lieut. Commanding 57th A.M.G.C.

WAR DIARY
or
INTELLIGENCE SUMMARY.
(Erase heading not required.)

Army Form C. 2118.

57 Bn MG Corps
Vol 6

Place	Date	Hour	Summary of Events and Information	Remarks and references to Appendices
LENS II 1/40,000 BOIS de WARNIMONT COIGNEUX BOIS d. WARNIMONT BUS ORVILLE	1/7/18		The Battalion was relieved in the line on the nights 14/15th and 27/3rd by the New Zealand Machine Gun Battalion. The troops that were relieved on the night 14/15th and Bn HQ remained at COUIN till the morning of the 17th when the whole Battalion marched to the BOIS de WARNIMONT. C Coy moved further forward into position on the purple reserve line in front of BEAUSSART - NEATRANCOURT - COURCELLES with their HQ in BUS. On the 1st Lieut A.A. GARDNER was admitted to hospital and struck off strength. On the 7th 2nd Lieuts F.S. STANDING and J. WHITON joined the Bn. and were posted to A and B Coys respectively. 46540 Sgt BULLOCK C. by was awarded the Meritorious Service Medal. 50307 Cpl. VINCENT D.Coy was awarded the Military Medal. On the 8th Lieut P.W. DEXTER TBy was evacuated to the Base and Lieut. H. Strople - 2nd Lieut V. ARCHIBALD joined the Battalion on the 10th and was posted to A Coy. 2nd Lieut H.C. HENRY was transferred to the Infantry on the 18th. The training programme for the period of rest included 3 days shooting for each Coy at ORVILLE. B Coy went on the 5th, D Coy on the 9th, C Coy on the 15th and A Coy on the 23rd. A Coy relieved C Coy in the purple reserve line on the 11th. During this period the division was the right reserve division of the IV Corps, holding in the 62nd Division. All reference divisions left for the south to 17th Division here in Cap Reserve. Dispositions therefor had to be altered - B Coy went into the CHATEAU de la HAIE switch with a section in front of LANCEY on the 14th. On the 14th Bn Scouts were held preparation to the Divisional Scouts on the 21st and 22nd:-	

Major F.T. Stormonth
O.C. 57 Bn

WAR DIARY or INTELLIGENCE SUMMARY

Army Form C. 2118.

Place	Date	Hour	Summary of Events and Information	Remarks and references to Appendices
LENS II 1/40,000 Bois de WARNIMONT	18/7/18		On the 18th 2nd Lieut. J.W. LEA joined the Bns and was posted to D.Coy.	
	21/7/18		The Divisional Sports were held on the 21st and 22nd. The Battalion won 1st in the grand aggregate competition, and won the Comic Vehicle with a donkey cart won "Officer who's knows a cow's udder and a donkey." The Bn entered for all competitions & won 1st in many. On the 26th 2nd Lieut A.A. BARDNER rejoined the Bn. The Battalion marched in and took over the 4th & 5th Line system of HEBUTERNE at the end of the month. This was cancelled and the 57th Div. ordered into the Byng reserve. The Battalion was relieved in takes Reserve by the 6th Bn. on the 29th and moved to BEAUDRICOURT.	
BEAUDRICOURT	28/7/18		2nd & 9th Regiment. Bn left on that day.	
GOUVES	29/7/18		On the 30th the Battalion moved to GOUVES in the XVIIth Corps in behalf of AMIENS. On the 31st the 57th Division commenced the relief of the 3rd and 4th Canadian Divisions E. of ARRAS. They had into the line first—during the 31st. The remainder of the Battalion stayed at GOUVES. The line was reconnoitred by the other Coys on the 31st, and further than were made for the take over the line on the 1st August.	
			Disposition of C. Coy as follows:- relieving the No.3 Coy 4th-5th Canadians in G.C. Coy H.Q. @ H1.c.8.8. Sheet 51.b. N.W. 1 sec. from hos. 29.30.31.32. 1 sec. C.H.U. & IMP. 1 sec. S.13. T.14. hos 33.34. 1 sec. 9.10.11.12.	
			Relief completed 11.46.p.m. no casualties	

Signed [signature]
Capt. Commanding C.

WAR DIARY or INTELLIGENCE SUMMARY

Army Form C. 2118.

Place	Date	Hour	Summary of Events and Information	Remarks and references to Appendices
DUISANS ARRAS	1/8/18		The Battalion was now in the XVII Corps commanded by Lieut-Gen. Sir Charles Fergusson Bt K.C.B, K.C.M.G. M.V.O. D.P. On August 1st A and D Coys moved into the line and B.Hq (& Reserve Coys) moved to DUISANS. On completion of relief dispositions were as follows Right Coy A Coy FEUCHY Sector Left " C " FAMPOUX NORTH Right " B " " SOUTH Left " D " " Bn HQ and B Coy DUISANS. During the relief No2 Pte Nimmo G A Coy was killed 33727 Sgt Parr H " was wounded and later died of wounds. DUISANS camp where B.HQ the Reserve Coy and 2i Echelon was located was a hut camp and in first class fettle therefore. The Hun itself was extremely quiet. Our own artillery fired good harassment but the enemy rarely retaliated except to carry out harassing fire on night targets using yellow cross gas shell. This caused a few casualties in A Coy on the 9th of the first shell importantly fallen in the mouth of the dug-out. The following were gassed:	
	9/8/18		24694 L/Sgt. Hornsby C.E. 116439 Pte. Mansfield W.J. 145193 Pte. Radcliffe W.L. 81870 " Hunt J 126834 " Hart W. 217089 " Way A.E. 37229 " Edmond W. 140229 " Lloyd J. 131423 " Jack G. 68847 " Athorn P. " Stamp J.	On the 5th 133143 Pte Jennings A.H was wounded (at duty) On the 7th 112089 Pte Wax, A.E. A Coy was wounded (at duty) Lieut was passed on the 9th Lt-Col [signature] commdg 5/1B. MGC

Army Form C. 2118.

WAR DIARY
or
INTELLIGENCE SUMMARY.
(Erase heading not required.)

Instructions regarding War Diaries and Intelligence Summaries are contained in F. S. Regs., Part II. and the Staff Manual respectively. Title pages will be prepared in manuscript.

Place	Date	Hour	Summary of Events and Information	Remarks and references to Appendices
DUISANS ARRAS	9/8/16		On the 9th Lieut C.V. Corpenel the Battalion and was posted to C Coy. late been transferred to D Coy. Lieut F.W. Wilkinson was attached from 1st Yorks Regt.	
	9/7/16		Bdn. relieved D Coy, night 9/10th in the famous Tooth Redt. D Coy in Bde reserve at DUISANS.	
	10/8/16		6143 Cpl Collinson W.V. Coy. was wounded.	
	14/8/16		Major W.A. Brereton D.S.O. proceeded to assume command of the 17th Bn M.G.C. and 2nd/Lieut. F.J. Emerson was admitted to hospital 14/8/16. The Division were warned that it would be relieved in the line by the 51st Division when the 1st and 19th One Brigade (the 170th) was to remain behind for the present. Also remaining with them. On relief the Division were to be one Bde, and the Bn, were one Coy, were to concentrate in the St-POL area.	
	16/8/16		Major J. Robin joined the Battalion and assumed the duties of 2nd in command. The night 16/17th the relief by the 51st Division began. Coy. was relieved that night and Bde, on the night 17/18th. Both Coys on relief moved to DUISANS.	
	17/8/16		On the 1st 2nd Lieut E.A. Wood was was admitted to hospital	
	19/8/16		The Battalion had been supplied to move on the 18th by light-railway to MANQUAY but then was cancelled owing to shortage of accommodation and Bn HQ, B,C,D Coys remained at DUISANS till the 23rd. During this period there was full moon and clear nights, every aircraft saw active bombing back areas.	
	21/8/16		On the 21st 2nd Lieut C.J. Almond was wounded by a piece of falling shrapnel from anti-aircraft guns.	
	22/8/16		Night 22/23rd A Coy was relieved by the 12th Life Guards Machine Gun Battalion at 170th Inf/M.G. Coy was relieved by the 17th Argyll & Sutherland Battalion.	
SOMARIN	23/8/16		On the 23rd the whole Battalion moved to SOMARIN.	

J.M. Robin Lt. Col.
Cmmdg. 57th Bn. M.G.C.

WAR DIARY
or
INTELLIGENCE SUMMARY
(Erase heading not required.)

Army Form C. 2118.

Place	Date	Hour	Summary of Events and Information	Remarks and references to Appendices
Pt. Maps Sheet 51B NW 1/10,000 Lens 2/100,000	18/9/16		Whilst the Battalion was at Doisans and A Coy still in the line the 170th Inf. Bde. Franch. Alg. were attacked South of the Scarpe on the night 16/19. One sub section of A Coy under 2nd Lieut A.S. SOOLE went over with the Brigade. A line was established in H.28.a and c with the guns protecting the right flank of the Brigade. No opposition was met. About 8 p.m. on the 19th three guns were removed to approximately H.26 c.6.8 and H.28 c.65:40. At 9 p.m. these guns went attached by the party of the enemy who were driven off. On the night of the 20/21st the 170th Inf. Bde. and the subsection of A Coy withdrew to their original line without incident.	
SOMARIN BAPAUME	24/9/16		On the 23rd the Battalion moved to BAPAUME. C Coy & crew attached to BAPAUME. C Coy & crew attached to 172nd Inf. Bde. and proceeded to BRETENCOURT. Those orders were cancelled on the march and C Coy	
BRETENCOURT RANJART			went to vicinity of RANJART. The 57th Division were began to be involved in the general advance from the SCARPE southwards.	
BLAIREVILLE	26/9/16		On the 26th the Battalion less C Coy (who were attached to the 172nd Inf. Bde. marched by night to BLAIREVILLE Wood arriving about 4:20 am on the 27th.	
MERCATEL			The same night C Coy moved to MERCATEL.	

J. Lal.
Cmdg. 54th Bn. M.G.C.

Army Form C. 2118.

WAR DIARY
or
INTELLIGENCE SUMMARY.
(Erase heading not required)

Instructions regarding War Diaries and Intelligence Summaries are contained in F. S. Regs., Part II. and the Staff Manual respectively. Title pages will be prepared in manuscript.

Place	Date	Hour	Summary of Events and Information	Remarks and references to Appendices
LENS 11 1/100,000 Sheet 51.B.S.W 1/20,000 BLAIREVILLE HENIN "MERCATEL" FONTAINE	27/11/16		On the afternoon of the 27th the Battalion received orders to relieve the 5/2nd Bn MGC in the line. B Coy had already moved to the vicinity of HENIN in T7a. On the night of the 27/28th the Battalion relieved the 5/2 Bn MGC with dispositions as shown in Appendix A (57th Div MGC Operation Order No 25) attached.	Appendix A.
	28/4/16		On the morning of the 28th C Coy commanded by Major N.L.S.G. MAWBERGH assembled with the 172nd Inf Bde behind FONTAINE. 1 & 2 Sections with Vickers under Lt F.M. ACKROYD and 2nd Lieut F.L. HEDCOCK in T4.b. 3 & 4 Section on pack under 2nd Lt E.W. BARDEN and 2nd Lt E.C. JONES at T5.b. The first objective of the Brigade's attack was VISC coulee - HOOP LANE - Sunken Road in VIDC - left boundary of division at V10.b.0.6. Second objective was HENDECOURT and AJENCOURT.	
		12.30/m	At Zero hour 12.30 hrs Nos 3 and 4 sections advanced with the Nuova Battalion the 1/8th Royal Munster Fusiliers. On the 1st objective being taken Nos 3 & 4 Sections prepared to consolidate and as the Infantry did not reach their second objective these sections took up positions in V14.d. and V9.c. respectively. Only Lt BARDEN's section front installed approximation of covering each section. They did a certain amount of firing on the night flank with the Munster Fusiliers during the attack as the 56th Division did not progress its offensive towards sent of 2nd Lt J.W. LEA's section of D Coy set on tracks to protect the exposed right flank from T7a & 36. This section came under heavy MG fire from LINCOLN RESERVE during its advance. No B 4906 L/c SAYLES did good work getting his rifle on.	

J.W. Mts. Lt-Col.
Comdg 57th M.G.C.

WAR DIARY or INTELLIGENCE SUMMARY

Army Form C. 2118.

Place	Date	Hour	Summary of Events and Information	Remarks and references to Appendices
MERICOURT - HENIN FONTAINE HENDECOURT	28/8/18		Loan in the plan to ensure the left flank against counter-attack the Officer Commdg. sent No 3 Section of D Coy under Lt A.E. GARDNER & position to PIO C 8.5. L Gardner had great difficulty in attaining except to protect his flank, but remained in this position throughout the operation — 28/29/30 August. Nos 1 and 2 Sections which were to the flank of the O.C.'s H as a mobile reserve were employed to consolidate as follows— No 1 Section. V.8.f. The Section in V.8.t. at the beginning of the attack Coys transportation had a short flank range by a German M.G. with hidden out in a hill on a FONTAINE village — The casualties however were only three annual slightly wounded. On the 29th the Coys dispositions were arranged as follows. No 1 (Capt. FAR ALLEY) V.14.f. — No 2 (Lt. Hope PLAYS) V.15.b. — No 3 Sect in Reserve V.8.f. — No 4 L.& F.Ors covering the right flank in position at V.8.f. f.6. —	M'guns on rooftops W/5 by 2/4 S.L Regmt.
	29/8/18		On the morning on the 29th D Coy commanded by Major H.A.T. MILLER relieved they commanded by Major C.H.B. SHEPHERD. Dispositions were as follows: — Coy. HQ. T.4b 2.5. — No. 1 Sect. 031.6.2.8. — No. 2 Sect.76b.6.2. — No.3 Sect.75b.6.4. — No. 4 Sect.V.2.a.9.2.	

J. Miller. Lt-Col.
Commdg. 59th Bn M.G.C.

Place	Date	Hour	Summary of Events and Information	Remarks and references to Appendices
LENS HOSGNE MERCATEL HENIN HILL FONTAINE HENDECOURT	29/4/17	1pm	At 1pm on the 29th the 70th Inf Bde attacked with objectives Kraut, O.23.d.9.3 enclosure – RIENCOURT SPUR O.18.a. No.1 & 2 Sections 3 Coy followed up the starting flank on the right's left flank refused – The Hbrs reached RIENCOURT & beyond. Heavy fighting took place in the village. During the evening however the King's Own were forced out of the village as they received no support – sustained very heavy casualties – Sgt Av. TARLTON's Section protected the withdrawal from the ridge in O.13.b. He fought his guns back to Eastern sword junction of POINTER ALLEY & GUN ALLEY where he remained during the night. This entailed a withdrawal an advanced guard of 1000 yds without infantry escort – a very fine performance. During this period Lt C.V. COX who commanded the section was returning back with his infantry – on the left & ascertaining the situation at HENDECOURT, his left flank being entirely in the air. In this work he received he was thanked in writing by the Officer Commdg forward troops. Lt. Col HEATHCOTE. During the attack the left flank of the Infantry on RIENCOURT SPUR was entirely in the air on the attack on HENDECOURT was not successful though some of the Infantry succeeded in establishing themselves north of the church. All infantry however with drew subsequent to the line of CEMETRY AVENUE. No 2 Section D Coy retired to cover the left flank from wife & sight of the road became involved in the withdrawal of the King's Own from RIENCOURT as dusk, stated...	

Army Form C. 2118.

WAR DIARY
or
INTELLIGENCE SUMMARY.
(Erase heading not required)

Place	Date	Hour	Summary of Events and Information	Remarks and references to Appendices
MERCATEL, FEMIN HILL, FONTAINE, HENDECOURT	30/9/18		In the counter-attack from RIENCOURT on the road morning of the 30th Bat. Lt Cox's Subs. and Lt K.P.V CARPENTER'S Section were in action for a considerable period from 6 a.y Hundred yards & short ranges and were largely instrumental in stopping the attack. Later accurate fire from guns caused considerable casualties to parties of hostile, the whole eight guns forming a gradual sufficient strong point. Five gun team covers under fire killed by enemy snipers. During the day much good work was done in supplying these gun with ammunition. A very critical forward slope, No. 43345 Sgt. RAMSEY & No. 133715 Pte KEELING particularly distinguished themselves in their duties, leading every party to the contested ground at end of the day. D Coys disposition at the end of the action were as follows:- No. 1 Section in U18 about junction of GOM POM, POINTER ALLEYS covering the right flank and No. 2 Sec in U18 about junction of SPANIEL & GOM ALLEY and junction of CRUX TRENCH and POINTER ALLEY covering the approaches to HENDECOURT – Lt Gardiner's section in U10.c – L/Cox's section in hand of O.C by about U15-b-285.	
	31st		About 3 pm the same day they Germans counter-attacked the Canadian troops on our left. Lt Gardiner's section from D10.c was able to greatly assist the Canadian as the advancing enemy offerred them excellent targets from 700 to 950 range on a forward slope. The guns were not made any further but the attack.	

31st October
January 1st 1918

WAR DIARY or INTELLIGENCE SUMMARY

Army Form C. 2118.

Place	Date	Hour	Summary of Events and Information	Remarks and references to Appendices
Ad Zeni / Mercatel Henin Hill Fontaine	30/8/18		During the night 30th Bn. Bn. moved up in close support ready to support the next attack, one platoon guarding each flank, Batt. now Coy. HQ in U.57.2.8.	
Hendecourt	31/8/18		On the 31st Aug. no event of importance took place. The day was spent in consolidation & when pushing groups of Bn. arrived at Jenken midn in U.10 c 60.60. Casualties during the period Sept 5 the 12 midnight 31st Aug. midnight 31st were as follows:—	

Killed
9 = Lieut. H REED A Coy 30/8/18
51307 Cpl Vincent D "
584E2 " Millward E "
55144 " Penn H W C "
108203 2/c Hanten R M D "
140263 Pte Williamson T B "

Wounded
81711 Mc Carr J H C " 31/8/18
67301 " Youens T O C " 29/8/18
48224 2/c Norman A C " 26/8/18 (at duty)
16677 Cpl Bitson E C " " (")
122819 Pte Torran G A
145084 " Thomas J C A 24/8/18
145074 " Page H N A
126704 " Evans P A
40682 " Miller M A
67179 " Cox H A A
143077 " Robinson J L A
148141 " Redhead W A
67245 " Dewhurst A C
146231 " Boddy F C 30/8/18
56217 M Matthews W C

Wounded (contd)
145223 Pte Prespet C Coy 30/8/18
24006 L/c Attwood J R Coy "
141141 Pte Duffey F R " 31/8/18
46632 " Lukey A D " "
74003 " Pheridan J B " "
127009 " Ford W " "
54217 Cpl Robinson A C " "

[signature]
Commdg. 9/7th M.G.C

a/4 A

Copy No. 17

SECRET   Date. 27/8/18.

Ref Sheet 51 b S.W.
57th BATTN M.G.C. OPERATION ORDER No. 25.

1. 57th BATTN M.G.C. will relieve 52nd Bn M.G.C. to-night.

2. INFORMATION. (a) The Canadian Corps are in possession of ridge in O 25 c and 33 Central, and are advancing. The 52nd Division are reported advancing in U 9 a and c. The 56th Division are reported advancing on BULLECOURT.

   (b) The Germans are reported to be still holding CROISILLES and the vicinity.

3. INTENTION. The immediate objectives of the Division are HENDECOURT and RIENCOURT. The advance will continue tomorrow.

4. DISPOSITIONS. (a) C Coy 57th Bn M.G.C. will be at the disposal of G.O.C. 172nd Brigade.

   (b) B Coy will move as under:-
   Hd Qrs to T 4 b. 7.3 at present occupied by D Coy 52nd Bn.
   Their guns will be disposed as follows:-
   To cover crossings in LA SENSEE RIVER and be prepared to support an advance from FONTAINE la CROISILLES by direct over-head fire.
   One section O 31 c - One section U 1 a - One section T 6 - One Section T 5 b.

   (c) O.C. B Coy will report to G.O.C. 170th Brigade and be under his orders in case of enemy counter-attack.

   (d) D Coy will move to pill box T 4 b 90.65 and will have one section to command southern slopes of HENIN HILL in T 5 c. One Section T 5 a. One section N 35 c. One Section at disposal of Coy Commander. This Coy will be in support under control of O.C.Bn. The Officer Commanding Coy will maintain touch with G.O.C. 170th Brigade, but will not be under his tactical control except in case of enemy counter attack.

   (e) A Coy will be in reserve in sunken road T 2 b.

5. Battn Hd Qrs will be at N 35 c S.R. Battn Hd Qrs will open at 9 a.m.

1.

6. ADMINISTRATIVE. (a) Coys will form forward dumps of ammunition from mobile reserve and send to Bn Hd Qrs for re-filling when necessary.

(b) Water. Coys will have at their disposal a water cart which should be re-filled at Bn Hd Qrs.

(c) Transport. (Fighting) O.C. Coys must use their own discretion as to the position of their fighting transport and whether an advance is to be carried out on limber or pack. 2nd Echelon Transport will move into the vicinity of B.H.Q. tomorrow.

7. MOVE COMPLETE will be reported by runner to Advanced Report Centre at Hd Qrs A Coy. The Bn Signals Officer will arrange this.

8. Dispositions will be sent as soon as possible.

9. Acknowledge.

_____ Capt & Adjt
87th Bn C.E.F.

Issued at

Distribution Copy No 1 87th Div (G)
2 A Coy
3 B "
4 C "
5 D "
6 82nd Bn C.E.F.
7 85th Bn C.E.F.
    2nd Canadian Div Bn C.E.F.
9 C.R.E.C.
10 172 Inf Bde
11 171 " "
12 172 " "
13 R.T.O.
14 M.O.
15 Q.M.
16/17 War Diary
18 File.

5-7 Bn M.G. Corps
968
Sep. 1918

On His Majesty's Service.

A.G. Office
3rd Echelon
Base

This packet contains nothing
but important official documents.

G.T. van ???
Lt. Colonel

[57th DIVISION "A" FRANCE stamp]

A.G. 3rd Echelon

Herewith War Diary for the
57 Bn M.G. Corps for Septr. 1918.

[signature]
Major General
Commanding 57 Division

27.10.18

H.Q. 57th Division (G)

> 57TH BATTALION
> MACHINE GUN
> CORPS
> No. MGR/8/739
> Date. 26/10/18.

Herewith War Diary for Septr., together with Appendices.

[signature]

Lt. Col.
Commandg 57th Bn. M.G.C.

Army Form C. 2118.

WAR DIARY
or
INTELLIGENCE SUMMARY.
(Erase heading not required.)

Instructions regarding War Diaries and Intelligence Summaries are contained in F.S. Regs., Part II. and the Staff Manual respectively. Title pages will be prepared in manuscript.

Place	Date	Hour	Summary of Events and Information	Remarks and references to Appendices
HENIN HILL FONTAINE HENDECOURT RIENCOURT	1/9/18	4.50 a.m.	On the 1st Septr. 171st Inf. Bde. attacked HENDECOURT with the 2/7th King's Own at 4.50 a.m. This attack was supported by No. 3 Section "C" Coy under 2/Lieut. R.W.Barber and No. 3 Sect. D. Coy under Lieut. A.A.Gardner. Considerable resistance was encountered in the South Eastern corner of HENDECOURT and from GREYHOUND AVENUE. 2/Lieut. Barber leaving 2 of his guns just north of the Hendecourt-Bullecourt Road in U.17.a. went forward himself with 2 guns. Both he and Sergt Eyles fought their guns at point blank range with great skill and courage. A German machine gun was put out of action at 30 yards range, casualties inflicted on the enemy, and time given for the infantry to re-organise on the road. Three of Sgt Eyles's team were wounded by snipers. Pte. McGibbon badly wounded in a most exposed situation. Pte Wilson pulled him under cover in a shell hole at great personal risk. On the gun withdrawing to the road Pte. Wilson remained with the wounded man alone for about a quarter of an hour nearly surrounded by Germans. Shortly afterwards Lieut. Barber with Private Wilson carried out the wounded man under heavy fire.	A44 A A/4 A(1)
	2/9/18		Having re-organised, the infantry again advanced and took the line of GREYHOUND AVENUE. The guns then got into position flanking HENDECOURT at U 17.a.6.2. Lt. Gardner's section got into position in the CHATEAU WOOD at U 11.d.9.1. behind the Canadians without much incident.	
		6.5. p.m.	At 6.5. p.m. the 2/6th Liverpool Rifles attacked RIENCOURT with the 6th Liverpool Irish in support. B Coy moved forward with them and helped to consolidate the village occupying positions in U 18.c.9.4. (2/Lt C.G.Tothill) U 13.b.5.0. (Lt. L.C.H.Chase) and U 17.d.7.3. (2/Lt J.Whiston). Coy Hd. Qrs with No. 1 Section in reserve moved to U 17.c.7.2. The reserve section was subsequently moved by the Officer Commdg. to U 24 c 4.5. to protect the right and exposed flank. During this operation the vicinity of the MOULIN SANS SOUCI was in the hands of the enemy and a good deal of machine gun and rifle fire came from that direction. The advance of B Coy was carried out under some difficulty owing to gas shelling, but all guns successfully reached their objectives with slight casualties. During the operation Nos. 1 & 2 sections of D Coy from U 18 d. gave valuable covering fire on the RIENCOURT RIDGE.	A44 B
	2/9/18	5 a.m.	At 5 a.m. on the morning of the 2nd. 172nd Inf. Bde. was ordered to assemble in U 11.b. and advance in a south easterly direction behind the Canadians until they reached the DROCOURT - QUEANT line in V 13 d. at this point the Royal Munster Fusiliers branched off mopping up the Drocourt-Queant system in square V 20.a and c, and the 2/4 S.L.R. the first system in	

WAR DIARY
or
INTELLIGENCE SUMMARY.
(Erase heading not required.)

Army Form C. 2118.

Instructions regarding War Diaries and Intelligence Summaries are contained in F. S. Regs., Part II. and the Staff Manual respectively. Title pages will be prepared in manuscript.

Place	Date	Hour	Summary of Events and Information	Remarks and references to Appendices
Alfred S.D.16 WEST O SE 1/20000 2/9/18				
HENDECOURT MENNERT			square V 15 a, b, and c, the general direction of this attack coming due South. The attack was supported by Tanks. To assist this operation and to protect the Brigade both during the time of its wheel and also after obtaining its objectives the following machine gun dispositions were made. A Coy commanded by Capt. D.C. Davis, M.C., with 5 sections on pack and 2 sections with limbers advanced through HENDECOURT and got his leading 2 sections in action in front of DACHSHUND AVENUE in square U 16 to traverse the DROCOURT - QUEANT line constantly during the Brigades advance. As soon as the progress of the rolling barrage admitted, 2/Lt. Archibald's section moved to positions in V 14 c. 3.6.and V 20 a. 7.4. to protect the left flank of the Royal Munster Fusiliers. 2/Lt. J.W.Ware's section moved up in support to V 15 a. 9.2. As the advance continued Lt. H.Dixon brought his section into action on either side of TURTLE TRENCH in U 16 c and also in EMU ALLEY and finally disposed his section and Lt. A.S. Soole's section in depth as follows:- 2 guns in V 16 b. 6.3. 2 " " V 16 a. 5.4. 2 " " U 18 c. 7.2. 2 " " V 16 c. 4.8. The whole operation was carried out most successfully, the forward sections obtaining good targets both for machine gun and rifle fire. The guns reached their objectives with slight casualties. Capt. Davis was severely wounded early in the operations and the Coy had 5 other casualties. During the operations the Officer Commandg sent Lieut. R.C. Jones's section and 6/Lt. F.L. Hedgcock's section of C Coy to positions in U 24 d. 5.3. and U 24 d. 2.2. to secure the right flank. The movement of all guns was carried out entirely according to plan and all guns reached their exact objectives. The 52nd Divn on the right advanced later in the day, and the situation on the right flank became settled. At about 10 a.m. the 63rd Naval Divn passed through the 172nd Bde. and advanced towards the line of the CANAL DU NORD having also taken PRONVILLE from the North. During the operations the guns were frequently without escort and the ammunition supply very	A.M.C. B.Blackwell Lt Col Commdg 171 M.M.C.
		10 a.m.		

Army Form C. 2118.

WAR DIARY
or
INTELLIGENCE SUMMARY.
(Erase heading not required.)

Instructions regarding War Diaries and Intelligence Summaries are contained in F. S. Regs., Part II. and the Staff Manual respectively. Title pages will be prepared in manuscript.

Place	Date	Hour	Summary of Events and Information	Remarks and references to Appendices
			difficult owing to lack of carriers but this difficulty was successfully overcome.	

Alfred Puckle Lt. Col.
Comdg. 17/M. MGC

A5834 Wt.W4973 M687 750,000 8/16 D. D. & L. Ltd. Forms/C.2118/13.

WAR DIARY
or
INTELLIGENCE SUMMARY.

(Erase heading not required.)

Army Form C. 2118.

Place	Date	Hour	Summary of Events and Information	Remarks and references to Appendices
SIISSWITSE ZONE SYGNF 1/20000	3/9/18		On Septr. 3rd the Battn concentrated as under:- At HENDECOURT - lez - CAGNICOURT in square U 17 and square U 23 a. and b. Battn. Hd. Qrs. at U 17 a. 3.3.	
HENDECOURT - CAGNICOURT			From the 6th to the 8th the time was spent in re-organising and re-fitting generally. During the period there was a good deal of shelling with high velocity shells in the Battn area. On the 6th inst. a shell pitched in "D" Company's mess, killing simultaneously Capt. H. Bushell, Lieut. A.A. Gardner, " R.P.V. Carpenter, " F.J. Standring, " E. Nisbet, 2/Lieut. H.N. White. 2/Lieut. J.W. Lea. and severely wounding	
INCHY EN- ARTOIS SECTOR	8/9/18 9/9/18		In the afternoon of the 8th and the night of the 8th/9th the Battn. relieved the 63rd Battn. in the INCHY - en - ARTOIS sector. "A" Coy under Major J.A.Barraclough, M.C., and "B" Coy under Major R.A.T. Miller went into the line on the right and left respectively with 171st Inf. Brigade. Dispositions as under:- "A" Coy Hd. Qrs. D 18 a. 7.2. 4 guns in D 18 a. 9.8. covering front and right flank 4 " " E 13 b. 2.3. covering front and right flank 2 " " E 7 c. 7.1. 2 " about E 13 a. 4.6. 2 " " D 12 c. 1.9. covering exits of INCHY "B" Coy Hd. Qrs. D 5 c. 9.5. 2 guns " D 5 a. covering North East 2 " " D 5 d. covering South East 2 " " D 6 d. 4.2. flanking INCHY 2 " " D 6 b. 8.7. flanking INCHY 2 " V 30 d. 6.2. covering front and left flank 2 " V 29 d. 9.8. covering front and left flank	

Alfred Webb Lieut Col
Commanding 57th Battn M.G.

WAR DIARY
INTELLIGENCE SUMMARY.
(Erase heading not required.)

Army Form C. 2118.

Place	Date	Hour	Summary of Events and Information	Remarks and references to Appendices
Sheet 57° N G 1/20000	9.9.18		4 guns W 20 c. 6.2. enfilading CANAL - DU - NORD "C" Coy in support Hd. Qrs. at D 4 c. 5.5. "D" Coy in reserve in square V 20 c. with the Battn. rear echelon. Battn. H.Q. in Quarry V 28 d. 0.0.	
	10.9.18		The relief was carried out without incident, except that No. 1 Section "B" Coy under Lieut. A.D.G.Brown was heavily shelled; Lieut. Brown was wounded and 4 other ranks. As the Section could not be approached in daylight being only some 200 yards from the German line on a forward slope, they could not be evacuated until the early morning of the 10th. The Section was then withdrawn.	
			On the night of the 9th/10th the Divisional boundary was extended to include MOEUVRES running along grid line E 19 c. 0.0. - E 21 c. 0.0. The 170th Inf. Brigade then took over the right sector and the necessary machine gun dispositions were made to cover this flank.	
			During the 9th and 10th various changes were made to use the machine guns to better advantage.	
MOEUVRES.	11/9/18		On the 11th inst. at 6.15 p.m. 57th Division were ordered to attack the line of the CANAL - DU - NORD, the 170th Brigade on the right and the 171st Brigade on the left. This operation necessitated the capture of MOEUVRES. Both Brigades were ordered if possible to exploit success and establish posts in the CANAL - DU - NORD line effecting a junction if possible in this line.	APP. D
			The 170th Brigade on the right attacking with the 1/5th North Lancs in front and the 2/4th North Lancs in support were successful in capturing MOEUVRES and reached the trench in the HINDENBURG Support Line running north and south through E 14 d. 8.0. A field gun was captured and about 90 prisoners. They found it impossible to reach the Canal bank. Both flanks were entirely in the air.	
			To support this portion of the attack 2 guns were moved to ROLANDS POST and No. 4 Section of "A" Coy under Lieut. H.J.D. Day was ordered to reach the Canal bank in E 21 a. and to enfilade it both north and south. Being unable to do this owing to the infantry being held up, Lieut. Day established himself and 2 guns at about E 14 d. 60.05 flanking	

Commanding 57th Battn M G

WAR DIARY
or
INTELLIGENCE SUMMARY.
(Erase heading not required.)

Army Form C. 2118.

Place	Date	Hour	Summary of Events and Information	Remarks and references to Appendices
Skull St Mk	12/9/18		the Canal to the south and protecting the right flank. Two guns under Sergt. L.G.Brook became separated in the fighting and eventually established themselves on the left flank of MOEUVRES in about E 14 c 5.0. An immediate counter-attack at about 8.15 p.m. was driven off successfully. To assist the 171st Brigade's attack, No. 4 Section "B" Coy under 2/Lieut. G.C. Tothill was ordered to proceed down HOBARD STREET and get into position on the Canal bank about E 8 d. 6.6. flanking the spur in E 9 c. to the north and south in conjunction with the 1/8th Liverpool Irish. The Company of the 1/8th Liverpool Irish were entirely unsuccessful, suffered heavy casualties, and retired to their original line. Being unable to proceed further, Lieut. Tothill remained about E 14 a. 2.8. until towards midnight in case of a counter-attack. A further attack was ordered but did not take place, and at dawn Lieut. Tothill established himself at E 13 b.2.2. One Company of the 1/8th Liverpool Irish reached its objective on the Canal bank but was forced subsequently to withdraw. The 2/7th K.L.R. attacked on the left and succeeded in establishing 2 posts on the Canal bank. Their left post however was forced to retire as they were taken in the rear, the Canadians having made no advance. One post however established itself successfully on the Canal bank in about E 2 d. 0.0. This operation was further supported by barrage fire from both "A" & "B" Companies throughout the operation. The infantry was subjected to heavy machine gun fire from forward positions and also from the banks of the CANAL - DU - NORD. On the 12th inst. the remains of the two Coys east of MOEUVRES endeavoured to consolidate their position then exposed on all flanks. Lieut. Day's section also consolidated where they could best protect the flanks of the infantry and 2 guns were moved to E 13 d. 3.5. in support and 2 guns under 2/Lieut.	

Commanding 57th Battn M.C.

WAR DIARY
or
INTELLIGENCE SUMMARY.
(Erase heading not required)

Army Form C. 2118.

Place	Date	Hour	Summary of Events and Information	Remarks and references to Appendices
Sauchy-Cauchy Zone	13/9/18	6.10 p.m.	Archibald to E 19 a. 7.4. and 2 guns to E 19 d. 3.9. to cover the Southern flank of MOEUVRES Village and the junction of the Guards Division and orders were issued to establish posts covering the flank in CEMETERY SUPPORT but this operation was not carried out.	App E
			In the evening at 6.10 p.m. the enemy bombardment of MOEUVRES became intense. The enemy were first seen by Lieut. Day at 6.35 p.m. and penetrated into the village at 8.10 p.m. The 2 guns under Lieut. Day came into action at close range on the Germans as they crossed the Canal bank. Being subsequently outflanked they withdrew, coming into action again about E 20 b. 2.9. but being again outflanked they withdrew to ruins near the cross roads E 14 d. 2.0. The Germans had then practically complete possession of the whole village. To avoid losing guns Lieut. Day had to withdraw due North into the open country eventually reaching HObart STREET just before dawn. He re-formed his section at about E 13 d. 9.6. at "Stand to" on the morning of the 13th.	
			- Lieut. Day was able to inflict considerable casualties on the enemy and also casualties were observed to be inflicted by 2/Lieut. Archibald's section firing 4,000 rounds direct with the aid of an artillery observer.	
			During the 13th our infantry again occupied the village the Germans having retired.	
	15/9/18 16/9/18		On the night of the 15th/16th the 172nd Inf. Brigade relieved the 171st Inf. Brigade. The 1st Royal Munster Fusiliers took over the protection of the northern flank of MOEUVRES establishing amongst others a post in E 14 central. This post which withstood one night's attack was subsequently withdrawn to the Red House in the northern outskirts of MOEUVRES. This post was again recaptured at 4 a.m. on the morning of the 16th and further posts established in the eastern end of CEMETERY SUPPORT. The co-operation of No. 1 section under Lieut. L.F.M. Ackroyd was arranged for by the Officer commanding the 1st Royal Munster Fusiliers.	
			"B" Company were relieved by "C" Company of the 52nd Battn on the night of the 15th/16th "A" and "B" Companies in support and reserve were also relieved by "B" & "D" Companies respectively.	
			"C" Coy relieved "A" Coy on the 13th/14th in the right sector. "C" Coy was relieved by	

Commanding 57th Battn. M.G.

Army Form C. 2118.

WAR DIARY
or
INTELLIGENCE SUMMARY.
(Erase heading not required.)

Instructions regarding War Diaries and Intelligence Summaries are contained in F.S. Regs., Part II. and the Staff Manual respectively. Title pages will be prepared in manuscript.

Place	Date	Hour	Summary of Events and Information	Remarks and references to Appendices
About 57 NE 2000	16/9/18		"A" Coy 52nd Battn. on the night of the 16th/17th.	
			Throughout this period constant harassing fire was continued both by day and by night upon the enemy's communications, Hd. Qrs. and centres of activity on the CANAL - DU - NORD.	
	17/9/18		During the night of the 15th/16th "A","B" & "D" Coys concentrated at NOREUIL, "C" Coy following on the 17th.	
			Throughout the period of these operations the enemy's shell fire increased considerably in volume. A considerable quantity of Blue X gas being used nightly in the Battery areas and both Blue & Yellow X on the forward areas. The vicinity of INCHY - en - ARTOIS was heavily shelled after our attack on the 12th and the vicinity of MOEUVRES village was shelled daily with considerable intensity.	
			The dispositions of the guns handed over were as follows:-	
			Left Coy:- 2 guns V 30 a. 8.0.	
			2 " V 30 d. 6.2.	
			4 " E 1 a. 3.4.	
			2 " D 6 d. 4.2.	
			2 " E 13 b. 3.1.	
			2 " E 7 d. 7.2.	
			2 " in reserve D 6 a. 50.45.	
			Right Coy:- 2 " E 13 a. 4.5.	
			2 " E 13 d. 3.5.	
			2 " E 13 c. 6.2.	
			2 " E 19 a. 6.4.	
			2 " E 19 d. 3.9.	
			4 " E 14 a. 4.0.	
			2 " in reserve at Coy H.Q.	

B. Webb ... Lieut. Col.
Commanding 57th Battn. M.G.C.

Army Form C. 2118.

WAR DIARY
or
INTELLIGENCE SUMMARY.
(Erase heading not required.)

Instructions regarding War Diaries and Intelligence Summaries are contained in F.S. Regs., Part II. and the Staff Manual respectively. Title pages will be prepared in manuscript.

Place	Date	Hour	Summary of Events and Information	Remarks and references to Appendices
Map Ref. Lens 11 1/100,000 57c.1/40,000 57c N.E. 1/20,000 MONCHIET.	8/9/18 12/9/18 13/9/18 17/9/18		On 8th Lieut. H.Dixon "A" Coy was admitted to Hospital. On 12th a draft of 21 O.R. arrived. On 13th 2/Lieuts F.Reynolds & W.Young joined the Battn. On 17th a draft of 33 O.R. arrived.	
	17/9/18		On the 17th the Battn. (less "C" Coy) moved to MONCHIET by train, "C" Coy following on the 18th.	APP F.
	18/9/18 to 26/9/18		The period 18/9/18 to 26/9/18 was spent in reorganisation, training and recreation. Route marches were made and an inter-sectional football competition was started.	
	20/9/18		On the 20th a draft of 10 O.R. arrived transferred from 63rd Battn.M.G.C.	
	22/9/18		On 22nd Lieut. W.Archibald was admitted to Hospital	
			On 22nd preliminary instructions were received that the XVII Corps in conjunction with Canadian and IV Corps would resume the attack.	
	23/9/18		Lieut.Col.J.F.R.Hope,.D.S.O. issued a Warning Order in connection with the attack and on the same date left to assume command of the 50th Inf. Bde.	APP. G.
	24/9/18		Lieut-Col B.H.Puckle,.D.S.O. assumed command of the Battn. Lieuts. L.G.Pinnell, R.Harris & E.R.Robinson joined on this date.	
NOREUIL.	25/9/18		The Battn. moved by train to VRAUCOURT and thence by march route to NOREUIL and bivouaced in Squares C 10. c & d. The Transport moved by road.	APP. H.
			"A" Coy 2/5 L.N.L.Regt (P) was attached for duty as carriers and reported on this date.	

.... Lieut Col
Commanding 57th Battn. M.G.C.

Army Form C. 2118.

WAR DIARY
or
INTELLIGENCE SUMMARY.
(Erase heading not required.)

Instructions regarding War Diaries and Intelligence Summaries are contained in F. S. Regs., Part II. and the Staff Manual respectively. Title pages will be prepared in manuscript.

Place	Date	Hour	Summary of Events and Information	Remarks and references to Appendices
PRONVILLE.	26/9/18.		On the 26th Instruction No. 1 in continuation of Warning Order of 23/9/18 was issued	APP J.
Map.Ref. 57c N.E. 1/20,000 57b N.W.	27/9/18 to 30/9/18	1.45.a.m.	The Battn. marched to Assembly area via LAGNICOURT & track S. of QUEANT & PRONVILLE	
PRONVILLE. MOEUVRES. ANNEUX. CANTAING. FONTAINE.- NOTRE- DAME. PROVILLE.			Details of the attack are given in Appendix K attached.	APP.K
			CASUALTIES during this period were as follows:-	
			KILLED. 116689. Pte. Crossley A.E. B. Coy. 27-9-18.	
			53974. " Miller J.H. " 28-9-18.	
			140729. Cpl. McAney P. A " 29-9-18.	
			156096. L/C. Tattersall T.C. D " 30-9-18	
			56735. Pte. Gardner C.F. D " "	
			2/Lt. Hedgcock F.I. " "	
			116264 L/C Moxham F. B " 29-9-18.	
			2/Lt. W. Pearson	
			DIED of WOUNDS. 122860. Pte. Smith J. D " 28-9-18.	
			WOUNDED. Capt. O. Greenwood C " 27-9-18 at duty.	
			7566. Pte. Proctor R.S. A " 29-9-18.	
			87610. " Rock A.S. B " 28-9-18. 58336. Pte Patching F C.Coy 27/9/18.	
			116486. " Cartwright W.F. " " 27-9-18. 133143. " Jennings J.S. D. " " 28/9/18.	
			145087. " Thrush H.H. " " 122813. " Mills F. " " 30/9/18.	
			116487. " Moss J. " "	
			6295. " Toombs W. C " 28-9-18 at duty.	
			ANIMAL CASUALTIES 17-9-18 to 30-9-18.	
			KILLED 1.R. 1.H.D. 5.L.D.M.	

.... Lieut. Col

Commanding 57th Battn. M G C.

Army Form C. 2118.

WAR DIARY
or
INTELLIGENCE SUMMARY.
(Erase heading not required.)

Summary of Events and Information

CASUALTIES during this period were as follows:-

KILLED
```
432223  Dvr.   Parr         W.          R.E.Sigs.   1-9-18.
136851  Pte.   Dean         R.G.        D. Coy.     2-9-18.
        Capt.  Bushell      H.            "         6-9-18.
        Lieut. Gardner      A.A.          "            "
          "    Standring    F.J.          "            "
          "    Carpenter    R.P.V.        "            "
          "    Nisbet       E.            "            "
        2/"    White        H.N.          "            "

30756   Pte.   Willis       S.          A   "      12-9-18.
67181   Cpl.   Lawrence     W.S.         "   "         "
```

WOUNDED.
```
103756  Cpl.   Parsons      B.          C   "       1-9-18.
133944  Pte.   Maddox       R.          "   "          "
140313   "     Forsberg     C.E.        B.H.Q.         "
 28124   "     Wilson       W.          B. Coy         "
 22781   "     McGibbon     J.          C.  "          "
 65358   "     Lake         R.          B.H.Q.         "    Since died of wounds 13-9-18.
        Capt.  D.C.Davis,M.C. A. Coy.                  "    at duty.
115604  Pte.   Noble        L.            "         2-9-18.
 58607   "     Overall      R.G.          "            "
128086   "     Green        J.            "            "
146776   "     Thomas       J.E.          "            "
 67211   "     Dolan        F.            "            "
 57001  Cpl.   Taylor       J.          B.  "       1-9-18.
  3277  Sgt.   Simpson      C.          A.  "       2-9-18. at duty.
 46900  Pte.   Stuart       A.W.        D.  "          "        "
```

Lieut Col

Commanding 57th Battn. M.G.C.

Army Form C. 2118.

WAR DIARY
or
INTELLIGENCE SUMMARY.
(Erase heading not required.)

Place	Date	Hour	Summary of Events and Information	Remarks and references to Appendices

WOUNDED.

54111	Pte.	Watson	W.	C. Coy.	1-9-18.	
	2/Lieut.	J.W.Lea		D. "	6-9-18.	
	Lieut.	A.D.G.Brown		B. "	8-9-18.	
65865	Pte.	Bates	W.	B. "	"	
83168	"	Mason	H,D.E.M.	B. "	"	
145289	"	Stenhouse	J.R.	" "	"	
140339	"	Kingston	A.E.	" "	"	
145135	"	Petty	E.J.	" "	"	
129293	"	Farthing	H.J.	" "	"	
44039	Cpl.	Bennett	J.	" "	10-9-18.	Died of wounds 13-9-18.
145189	Pte.	Williams	J.H.	A "	12-9-18	
142876	"	Graham	J.	" "	"	
59015	"	Rushton	F.C.	C "	13-9-18	
58050	Cpl	Jones	J.O.	" "	"	
146831	Pte	Reilly	T.T.	" "	"	
145167	"	McHugh	J.T.	" "	"	
105109.	"	Robinson	T.S.	" "	"	
145171.	"	Stevenson	S.S.	" "	"	
67049	"	Grant	J.	" "	"	
71919	"	Bradwell	S.A.	" "	"	
127330.	"	Barker	J.B.	" "	14-9-18.	
148193.	"	Askew	T.	B.H.Q.	13-9-18.	at duty.

ANIMAL CASUALTIES. 1-9-18 to 17-9-18.

Casualty.	R.	H.D.	L.D.H.	L.D.M.
Killed.	4	-	13.	2.
Evac. to M.V.S. wnd.	1	1	1	4.
Missing.	2.	-	-	1.
Total.	7.	1	14.	7.

.... Lieut. Col
Commanding 57th Battn M.G.C.

Ref Map 51 B.S.W. & 51 B.S.E. 1/20,000   Copy No. 6.
                                          31/8/18.

57th BATTN M.G.C. OPERATION ORDER No. 26.

1. INFORMATION   (a) The 56th Division hold the Factory in U 22 on line of sunken road to BULLECOURT.
   The Canadians hold line of CEMETERY AVENUE.

2. (1) 171st Infantry Brigade attacks tomorrow at 4.50 a.m.

   INTENTION Objectives GREYHOUND AVENUE U 12 c 2.0 to U 17 b. 2.2. thence to U 17 d. 9.3. and line of TERRIER ALLEY. Canadian 1st Division attack and hold CROW'S NEST and HENDECOURT CHATEAU simultaneously.

   (2) At 7 p.m. the 171st Inf. Bde attack RIENCOURT and RIENCOURT RIDGE and consolidate along line DACHSHUND AVENUE – EMU ALLEY to cross roads in U 23 d. 90.25. Map showing Infantry dispositions is issued herewith.

   (3) RIENCOURT RIDGE must be held.

3. DISPOSITIONS First Operation. C Coy will send one section to about U 17 a. 7.1. to flank eastern edge of HENDECOURT in first operation and will remain in that vicinity.
   D Coy will send one section to vicinity of U 17 b 5.9. to flank CHATEAU and ROAD and cross fire with guns in U 17 c. 7.1.
   These sections will not move until leading infantry are established but must be in close touch with them.

4. DISPOSITIONS Second Operation. B Coy will be prepared to move forward to consolidate RIENCOURT and RIDGE as under
   4 guns about U 17 c 8.5 firing N.E. covering slopes of ridge.
   2 guns U 18 c 8.3 firing N.E & E.
   2 guns U 18 c 8.25 flanking village to S.
   4 guns U 23 b 5.0 firing S.E. & S.
   4 guns in control of O.C. Coy at U 23 a. 70.97.
   Coy Hd Qrs will go forward to U 17 c 52.15 as soon as RIENCOURT is captured.
   Hd Qrs of C Coy will be at U 8 b 2.8.
   Hd Qrs of D Coy will be at U 15 b. 3.8.
   Hd Qrs of B Coy will be at U 15 b. 3.8. until moving forward.
   A Coy will relieve B Coys section U 10 c. 7.6 during night 1/2nd. They must be in position before dawn. One section move to U 8 central, One section to U 2 d. 8.05. The O.C. Coy will exercise his discretion as to when to move.

5. Bn Hd. Qrs will be with 171 Brigade at T 6 b 1.1.

6. Armourers with 2 spare guns will be at C Coy H.Q. U 8 b 2.8.

                                    (sgd) T.N.F. Wilson, Capt.
Copy No. 1 Filed   Adjt 57th Bn. M.G.C.
        2 57 Divn (G)
        3 170th Inf. Bde.
        4 171   "   "
        5 172   "   "
        6 War Diary.
        7 O.C. A Coy
        8 O.C. B "
        9 O.C. C "
       10 O.C. D "

SECRET.   31/8/18.

57th BATTN M.G.C. WARNING ORDER.

Ref. 51 B.S.W. 1/20,000

1. (a) The 171st Infantry Bde. will attack and hold RIENCOURT and HENDECOURT villages.
   (b) Date and Zero time will be notified later.

2. (a) B Coy 57th Bn. M.G.C. will be prepared to go forward with the 171st Inf. Bde. and occupy positions as shown roughly on map which will be issued later.
   Coy H.Q. to U 17 c. 52.17.
   4 guns at disposal of Coy Commander in position TERRIER ALLEY about U 23 a. 7.9.
   4 guns junction of BULLDOG SUPPORT and OSTRICH AVENUE U 23 b. 5.0 firing South and South East.
   2 guns about U 18 c 8.3. flanking village to South.
   2 guns DACHSHUND AVENUE U 18 c 6.3. firing North East.
   4 guns U 17 d. 8.5. sweeping northern spurs of RIENCOURT RIDGE.

   (b) O.C.Coy will arrange direct with the Brigade for carriers required.
   (c) O.C."C" Coy will move four reserve guns to U 17 a. 8.2. flanking Eastern side of HENDECOURT VILLAGE

3. (a) O.C.Reserve Coy will relieve B Coy's section in U 10 c on night prior to operations. They will be required to barrage road crossing U 12 c to U 12 central.
   (b) O.C.Reserve Coy will also be required to barrage the Crows Nest and will reconnoitre positions in U 10 c for this purpose at about 2,000 yards from objective.
   (c) After the operation he will withdraw three sections to positions in CRUX TRENCH U 9 a 1.7 and CEYLON TRENCH U 8 central keeping four guns at his disposal.

4. It is most important that every man in the sections going forward should be given on the ground some objective to go to.

5. Carefuly reconnaisance will be made with glasses.

6. Dumps and fire positions for barrage will be prepared on night 31st Aug /1st Sept and a plentiful supply of water and oil ensured.

7. Acknowledge (Coys only)

                                                      (Sgd) T.N.F.Wilson, Capt.
                                                            Adjt 57th Bn. M.G.C.

Ref map 51 B S.W. & 51 B S.E. 1/20,000   Copy No 1

APP B

1/9/18.

WARNING ORDER

1. Tomorrow the 1st Canadian Division attack from line roughly U 18 Central to V 1 a Central.
   OBJECTIVE. CAGNICOURT. Their right flank to be a straight line drawn from U 18 c 8.3. to V 21 a. 4.7.

2. The 172nd Inf. Bde will form up in square U 8 to-night. They will be prepared to advance in echelon to-morrow morning to guard the right flank of the Canadian Corps, and to mop up behind them.
   First Objective, the line from V 14 d. 4.0 to V 19 b. 8.0 and thence down the DROCOURT QUEANT support line.
   Second Objective, Cross roads in V 21 b. V 21 d. 0.0 V 26 d. 8.0.
   A Coy 87th Bn. M.G.C. will be prepared to advance acting in conjunction with this Brigade. Further details will be issued later.
   They will concentrate at once in square U 4 d.

3. Provided that the RIENCOURT RIDGE is successfully captured and consolidated, O.C. B Coy 87th Bn M.G.C. will employ his whole Coy on the Ridge to assist the advance of 172nd Bde. Detailed dispositions will be issued later.

4. C Coy 87th Bn. M.G.C. will be prepared to move through B Coy in an easterly direction forming a defensive flank in squares U 24 b and V 19 a. b. c. This will be carried out by advancing successive sections echeloned in depth.
   Should the advance be continued to the second objective C Coy will be prepared to continue the flank roughly on the line HIPPO LANE – WOMBAT LANE – and square V 26 a. B Coy in this case will form flank to first objective. Coy Hd Qrs at U 26 b. 70.30

5. D Coy 87th Bn M.G.C. will take over dispositions of C Coy's Section in U 17 a. to-night with their reserve section. Should the advance be successfully accomplished, they will concentrate in MORGAN TRENCH square U 17 c. taking over the Hd Qrs of B Coy in U 17 c. 68.18. They will be a reserve in the hands of Battn. Commander. On the relief of C Coy's section, C Coy's section will go into reserve by their Coy Hd Qrs.

6. The advanced Battn Hd Qrs will be with the Hd Qrs of the reserve Coy.

7. Should the attack on RIENCOURT be unsuccessful, the 170th Inf. Bde will be employed in its capture, the 172nd Inf. Bde still operating on the Canadian flank. C Coy 87th Bn M.G.C. might in this case be employed in assisting 170th Inf. Bde.

8. The 63rd Division should pass through the Division on the night 2/3rd Septr. Coys will withdraw as the tactical situation permits and concentrate Henin Hilland vicinity of Bn. Hd. Qrs U 34 d. Central.

9. Acknowledge

Distribution
  Copy No 1 File
       2 57 Div (G)   5. 172 Inf. Bde
       3 170 Inf Bde   6 A Coy
       4 171   "   "   7 B "
                        8 C "
       (O Bin Diary)   9 D "

T.W.Wilson
Adjt 87 Bn MGC

File App C
 9
 2/8/18.

Ref Map 51 B.S.W. & 51 B.S.E. 1/20,000.   Copy No. 12

57th BATTN. M.G.C. OPERATION ORDER NO. 27.

Reference Warning Order already issued.

1. **INFORMATION.** The 172nd Brigade will form up on the line of CEMETERY AVENUE in square U 11 c. A Coy will form up immediately in the vicinity of them. Forward Section Commanders will get touch with their respective Battalions the 1st Royal Munster Fusiliers in front, the 2/4th S.L.R. behind.

   1st PHASE. They will move off independently to the following positions, obtaining infantry escort or with the supporting infantry:-

   Left forward section to about U 18 a. 6.3.
   Right forward section U 18 c 5.7., and when situation admits to U 18 d. 9.0 in sub-sections.
   These Sections will traverse the DROCOURT-QUEANT line in V 13 d. and V 19 a. protecting the forward movement of the Brigade just north of the Divisional boundary.

   2nd PHASE. On reaching square 13 b. the Brigade wheels southwards, the 2/4th S.L.R. mopping up the front line system in square 19, the 1st Munsters the support line system in square 20. To protect this wheel, carefully observing the rolling barrage and moving behind it, left section will move to position in V 14 c 5.5. and V 20 a. 7.3.

   As the rolling barrage advances and the tactical situation admits, the right flank section will advance to V 18 d. 7.0 and V 18 d. 9.0 and thence to V 19 b. 60-25 and V 19 c 6.1. This will be the final position.

   The reserve sections will move forward in the hands of the Coy Commander to DACHSHUND AVENUE when clear of the forward sections. After that they will be used in accordance with his own initiative.

   Capt. Corsellis will act as liason Officer with the Bde. Bde Hd Qrs will be U 9a. 5.0.

   The reserve Battn. will form up in square U 9 d. and move to DACHSHUND TRENCH.

   Should the situation at dawn permit of releasing more guns, C Coy will send 2 sections one from U 15 b and one from reserve forward through B Coy to position in RIENCOURT TRENCH U 24 d. 70.35 to cover southern flank. Hd Qrs C. Coy U 15 b 2.8.

   O.C. B Coy will move his reserve section to vicinity of U 24 c. 4.6. and establish Coy Hd Qrs at U 23 b. 75.28.

2. Forming up place O 31 c. 2.7.

3. Time of moving forward 2 a.m.

4. ROUTE - CHERISY - HENDECOURT.

Capt & Adjt.
57th Battn. M.G.C.

Issued at 1.30 a.m
Distribution -
Copy No. 1 57 Div C   9 & 63 Bn MGC
     2 172 Inf Bde   10/11 War Diary
     3 171   12 File
     4 170
     5 A Coy
     6 B
     7/8 C

App D

SECRET.

Ref. Map 57 C N.E. 1/20,000.   Copy No. 12

Date 11/9/18.

57th BATTN M.G.C. OPERATION ORDER No. 22.

1. **INFORMATION.** Co-operating with attack further south by 4th and 6th Corps, 57th Division will attack and capture the Canal Bank within Divisional boundaries this evening. They will endeavour to exploit success to trench junction in N 9 c 10.86 to trench junctions N 15 b. 3.0. N 15 d. 35.20, N 21 b 30.85 and mop up CANAL DU NORD line between those points.
The 2nd Canadian Division is ordered to get touch with left flank of 171st Brigade on Canal Bank.

2. **INTENTION.** A and B Coy will assist the 170th Brigade on the right and the 171st Brigade on the left, each Coy sending a forward section to co-operate with the infantry and consolidate the line of the Canal Bank.

3. No. 4 Section B Coy under 2/Lt. Tothill will report to O/C 1/8th Liverpool Irish this afternoon at N 13 a. 2.8.
He will follow the advance of this Battn, using his own judgment as to line and time, and getting into position 2 guns about Canal bank in N 8 d. 2 guns shooting either side of spur in N 8 c.
No. 4 Section A Coy under Lieut. Day will report to O/C 1/5th L.N.L. Regt. this afternoon and act as above, getting his guns into position about N 15 c 3.3. 2 guns N 21 a. 2.7. flanking either side of the HINDENBURGH SUPPORT LINE.
2 guns of Lt. Bare's Section in N 13 a. will move to ROLAND POST in N 7 d. as soon as possible to be in position by 6 p.m.

4. (a) O/C B Coy will arrange to barrage the following points:-
Vicinity of CHATEAU BAINS - les - MARQUION throughout the operation.
Trench in N 2 d. from N 2 d. 9.4. to N 2 b. 8.0.
Fork roads and dug-outs in N 3 c and WARTBURG STRONG POINT in N 8 d. for 4 minutes, lifting to dug-outs from N 9 a 4.6. to N 3 c 25.20.

   (b) O/C A Coy will arrange to barrage 1st trench junction in N 9 c 10.86 for 4 minutes, lifting to vicinity of STRONG POINT in South West corner of QUARRY WOOD. Vicinity round trench N 21 b. and d. and enfilade barrage on sunken road between N 21 c 5.3. to N 21 d. 2.0.

5. ZERO HOUR will be 6.15 p.m.

6. Watches will be synchronised at 4 p.m. to-day by telephone. O/C Coys will arrange that their Section Commanders are provided with synchronised watches.

7. Artificers and 4 spare guns will be at Battn Hd. Qrs.

1.

8. O/C D Coy will have his animals harnessed and limbers in fighting order at 5.30 a.m. 18th inst. and having "stood to" will place all arms and equipment in immediate readiness and await orders.

9. O/C C Coy will report to Battn Hd. Qrs at 8 p.m. to-night.

                                        _____ Capt &
                                        Adjt. 57th Bn. M.G.C.

Issued at 5.30 p.m.

Distribution -

    Copy No. 1 57th Divn (G)
             2 170th Inf. Bde
             3 171st   "   "
             4 172nd   "   "
             5 1/8th Liverpool Irish
             6 1/5th L.N.L.R.
             7 A Coy
             8 B "
             9 C "
            10 D "
         11/ 12 War Diary
            13 File.

2.

SECRET.

Map Ref. 57 C. N.E. 1/20,000
        51 B S.E. 1/20,000

Copy No. 12
Date 14/9/18.

57th BATTN M.G.C. OPERATION ORDER No. 30.

1. The 57th Division will be relieved in the line by the 52nd Division between Septr. 15th and Septr. 17th.

2. 52nd Battn. M.G.C. will relieve 57th Battn. M.G.C. on nights 15th/16th & 16th/17th Septr.

3. On night 15th/16th
   (a) 1. C Coy 52nd Battn. M.G.C. will relieve B Coy 57th Battn. M.G.C. in left sector Divisional front.
        2. B Coy 52nd Battn. M.G.C. will relieve A Coy 57th Battn. M.G.C. in support.
        3. D Coy 52nd Battn. M.G.C. will relieve D Coy 57th Battn. M.G.C. in reserve in V 20 c.

   (b) Night of 16th/17th A Coy 52nd Battn. M.G.C. will relieve C Coy 57th Battn. M.G.C. in right sector of Divisional front.

4. All details of relief will be arranged between O/C Coys concerned.

5. On relief Coys will concentrate in an area to be notified later.

6. The command of the sector machine guns passes on completion of relief.

7. Advance parties consisting of one officer per company will report to the 2nd i/c at 9 a.m. to-morrow at Rear Battn Hd. Qrs. V 20 c to reconnoitre the area in which the Battn will concentrate.

8. Relief complete will be reported by Coys to Battn. Hd. Qrs. by code word of 3 letters beginning with the Coy letter stating time and casualties (if any).

Issued at 6.45 p.m.

Distribution - Copy No. 1 57 Div (G)
                 2 A Coy
                 3 B "
                 4 C "
                 5 D "
                 6 170 Inf. Bde.
                 7 171 " "
                 8 172 " "
                 9 52nd Bn.M.G.C.
               10 Guards Bn M.G.C.
               11 2nd Canadian Bn.M.G.C.
             12/13 War Diary.
               14 File.

W.T.Wilson   Capt & Adjt
57th Bn. M.G.C.

A. Coy.
B "
C "
D "

11/136
15/9/18

    Reference 57th Battn. M.G.C Operation Order No. 30. para. 5.

1. The Battn. will concentrate at NOREUIL.

2. Maps other than those on which information regarding the Divisional sector has been marked will not be handed over on relief.

(Signed). Y.R.F. Wilson Capt. & Adjt.
57th. Battn. M.G.C

App. 2. Copy No. 10.

16th Sept./18

Secret
Ref. Lens 11 1/100,000

57th Bn. M.G.C. Operation Order No. 31.

1. The Batt'n (less C Coy) will move to MONCHIET by train tomorrow. Entraining Station. BOYELLES Detraining Station. LAHERLIERE

2. The B'n (less C Coy) will move to BOYELLES to entrain tomorrow as in para 3 below.

3. (a) <u>Order of March.</u> B.H.Q B, A, D Coy

   (b) <u>Starting Point</u> Cross Roads. 200 yds East of L in NOREUIL

   (c) <u>Time</u> 9.30 am.

   (d) <u>Dress</u> Battle Order. Greatcoats will be carried in fighting limbers

   (e) <u>Route</u> ECOUST, CROISILLES, BOYELLES
   100 yards interval will be kept between Companies.

4. O/C D. Coy will detail one Officer to report to Representative of the Divisional Staff at BOYELLES at 12 noon & one officer to reconnoitre the route and report to the Adjutant before the Bn. moves

5. C. Coy will entrain at BOYELLES on the 18th Sept. at 2 p.m. They will arrive at the entraining station at 12 noon and will detail one Officer to report to a representative of the Divisional Staff at that hour. They will halt and form up prior to entrainment at the North side of the Railway.
Destination MONCHIET
Detraining Station. LAHERLIERE.

Distribution.
Copy No 1. 57 Div (G.)
    2 172 Inf. Bde
    3   A. Coy
    4   B "
    5.   C "
    6   D "
    7   Sec. do
    8   S.O.
    9   War Diary
   10   do.

Y.R.J. Wilson (Signed)
Capt. & Adjt.
57th Bn. M.G.C.

SECRET

Ref. Map 57 C.N.E. 1/20,000

No. MGR/8/467 Copy No. 9
Date 23.9.18

57th Battn. M.G.C. WARNING ORDER.

App G

1.   An attack will take place by the Canadian Corps, XVII Corps and the VI Corps.
        The First Objective of the XVII Corps will be taken by the 52nd Division and the 63rd Division.
        The Second Objective will be taken by the 63rd Division.
        These attacks will take place in conjunction with the 3rd Division on the right and the 4th Canadian Division on the left.

2.   The 57th Division will pass through the 63rd Division on the Second Objective and capture the Third Objective, and exploit success by seizing the crossings over the CANAL DE L'ESCAUT. This operation will be carried out in conjunction with the 1st Canadian Division on the left and the 2nd Division on the right.
        The Canadian main attack will be on the high ground north of FONTAINE round the Northern end of BOURLON WOOD. One Battn. will move through the Southern end of the Wood in conjunction with the 57th Division.
        171st Brigade will attack FONTAINE, 172nd Brigade CANTAING. 170th Brigade will be in reserve and be prepared to exploit success moving to Valley west of ANNEUX. The 171st Brigade with one Battn 172nd Brigade will move direct on its Objective, the Battn 172nd Brigade turning Southwards on reaching CANTAING TRENCH and Support.

3.   Brigades will assemble about HINDENBURG front line in about D 18. 17. 16. 171st Brigade leading.
        57th Battn. M.G.C. will assemble:- B Coy in square D 16 c, D Coy in square D 22 a. C Coy in Square D 21 b. A Coy in Square D 15 d. They will move forward via main BAPAUME-CAMBRAI ROAD, and all tracks will be reconnoitred from points of assembly to this road. This to be carried out at once.

4.   B Coy will act in conjunction with 171st Brigade, D Coy with 172nd Brigade, C Coy will be in support, and A Coy in reserve.
        The O.C. Battn. will be with Divisional Hd. Qrs. at D 17 a. 1.1.
        Each Coy will send one Officer to remain there until the order to move is given by the O.C.

5.   To assist the initial attack B Coy will send one section

1.

about F 19 c. 9.3. One section about F 25 b. 5.0. to traverse the CANTAING LINE whilst the 172nd Brigade moves down it, retaining two sections in E 30 a. The Coy Commander himself will watch the progress of the 171st Brigade and as soon as it is possible move his two remaining sections one section to Railway bank in F 15 a. 9.7. (2 guns to shoot north and 2 guns south of the Railway) and one section to about F 22 c 2.9. As soon as the situation permits O.C. B Coy will move section from about F 25 b. to about F 16 a. 3.2. and one section with his Hd. Quarters to about F 21 c. 4.1. and F 20 b. 9.1. denying exits to village.

6. D Coy will move 2 sections as far forward on the southern end of the ANNEUX RIDGE as the situation permits to protect the advance on CANTAING, endeavouring to reach positions about F 26 c 3.1. and L 2. d. 4.2. enfilading the village. His ability to move forward will depend on the progress of the direct attack on the village with which the closest touch must be kept, every opportunity being taken to assist the attack by over-head or flanking fire. He will keep 2 sections in readiness in square E 29 d. As soon as the situation permits he will move these forward to the following positions:- about F 25 a. 8.4. flanking spur and denying entry to village. L 4 a. 3.0. flanking village. He will move his Hd. Qrs. and section from F 25 c to F 26 d. 7.6.

7. C Coy will move to vicinity of E 29 a. The O.C.Coy will immediately get into touch with the advance of the 171st Brigade on FONTAINE and as soon as possible move one section to about F 20 c 4.6. and one section to about F 26 b. 2.6. to support the attack on FONTAINE village. The time when these sections can move must depend on the progress southwards of the 172nd Brigade. When B and D Coy have moved forward, C Coy will move their two remaining sections one section to F 26 a. 3.1. one section and Hq. Qrs. to F 25 b. 3.0.

8. A Coy will move in rear throughout first assembling at about E 28 c. They will subsequently move to E 30 a. One Officer will remain at Bn. Hd. Qrs. until the move. They will receive their orders to move from Bn. H.Q. They will hold themselves in readiness to exploit success with 170th Brigade covering the crossings over the CANAL DE L'ESCAUT.

9. Officers Commanding Companies will take immediate steps to see Brigadiers concerned. They will ascertain exactly the dispositions of the Infantry, and Section Commanders will see the Battn. Commanders with whom they are acting. The closest touch

must be kept throughout.   Escort where necessary will be arranged.

10.   The Battn. 2nd Echelon with 3 limbers per Coy will move forward in the vicinity of Divisional Hd. Qrs.   The 2nd i/c will be responsible for the supply of water, ammunition and rations, and for keeping touch with the Coys.

11.   Every Coy Hd. Qrs. will be marked by a flag of the Coy colours.

12.   Communications.   The Battn. Signal Officer will arrange rear communications in conjunction with the Divisional Signalling Coy, and communications forward to Coys by runners and visual.   He will maintain touch with the Battn. 2nd Echelon at all times.   Mounted orderlies will be attached to the Battn.

13.   Battn. Hd. Qrs. will be with the Division before Zero hour. They will move forward to close proximity of the Hd. Qrs. of the 171st and 172nd Brigade.

H.A.Oakeshott
Lieut. A/Adjt.
57th Battn. M.G.C.

ISSUED at 4 p.m. 23/9/18.

Distribution -
    Copy No. 1. 57th Divn (G)
           2. 170th Inf. Bde.
           3. 171st   "   "
           4. 172nd   "   "
           5. A Coy.
           6. B Coy.
           7. C Coy.
           8. D Coy.
           9. 2nd i/c
          10. S.O.
          11. R.T.O.
          12 File.
      13/ 14 War Diary.

Ref. Map. 57c. 1/40,000.   Copy No. 9.
                                            Date. 24/9/18.

App. H

57th BATTN. M.G.C. OPERATION ORDER No. 32.

1. The Battn will move to the vicinity of NOREUIL by train to-morrow.
    Entraining Station: BEAUMETZ.
    Detraining Station: VRAUCOURT.
    They will bivouac in Square C.10.c.&d.

2. The Battn will move to BEAUMETZ to entrain to-morrow as in para. 3 below.

3. (a) Order of March. H.H.Q. D. A. C. B. Coys.
   (b) Starting Point. Opposite B Coy Officers Mess.
   (c) Time. 5.0.p.m.
   (d) Dress. Battle Order. Greatcoats rolled will be carried in the fighting limbers.
   (e) 100 yards interval will be kept between Coys.

4. O.C. A Coy will detail one Officer to report to the Station at 5 p.m. and one Officer to reconnoitre the Route and report to the Adjutant before the Battn. moves.

5. An advance party consisting of one Officer and one N.C.O. per Coy and one Officer and 2 N.C.O's Bn.Hd.Qrs. will parade with bicycles at B.H.Q. at 7.0.a.m. to proceed by the 8.40 train from SAULTY.
    A guide will be sent to the detraining point at VRAUCOURT by 7.0.p.m.

6. Packs. Packs and surplus stores and kits will be taken to the Q.M.Stores by 12 noon.

7. Dixies. 9 dixies per Coy will be carried, and a hot meal will be provided with Cookers on arrival.

    Coy Q.M.Sergeants will report to the Q.M.Stores with bicycles at 8.30 a.m.

8. Tents. All tents will be returned to the Q.M.Stores, Divisional Reception Camp, by 10.30 a.m. and receipts obtained.

9. Transport. Battn. Transport will proceed by road under the Bn. Transport Officer as follows:-
   (a) Order of March. B.H.Q. D. A. B. C. Coys.
   (b) Dress. Battle Order.
   (c) Starting Point. B Coy's Officers Mess.
   (d) Time 10 a.m.
   (e) Route. BRETENCOURT - BLAIRVILLE - BOISLEUX - AU - MONT - ST LEGER - CROISILLES - NOREUIL.
   (f) Water. 2 hours halt for water at BOISLEUX - AU - MONT.
   (g) Water Carts will be filled.
   (h) 100 yards interval will be kept between each Coy Transport.

                        (Sd) H.A.Oakeshott. Lieut A/Adjt.
                             57th Bn. M.G.C.

Issued at 11.55.p.m.
Distribution-
    Copy No. 1 57 Divn (G)
         2 A Coy.   9/10 War Diary.
         3 B "
         4 C "
         5 D "
         6 B.T.O.
         7 Q.M.
         8 File

Secret

APBJ

Ref. Map 57 C.N.E. 1/20,000   Copy No. 14

57th BATTN M.G.C. INSTRUCTION ~~ORDER~~ No. 1.

in continuation of Warning Order 23/9/18.

1. As in Warning Order.

2. As before as in Warning Order.

3. Coys will assemble as in Warning Order.

     (a) ROUTE.   South of Southern Trench of HINDENBURG Front Line and within the Divisional Area.
     (b) TIME:- to follows 172nd Inf. Bde. Not to commence before Zero minus four hours and to be completed by Zero hour.

4. As in Warning Order. Divisional Hd. Qrs. will be at D 17a. 8.2

5. " " " " "

6. " " " "

7. " " " "

8. (as ~~before~~) *Warning Order.*   On reaching the 3rd Objective, if no† opposition is met with, 171 and 172 Inf. Bdes will seize the crossings of the CANAL - DE - L'ESCAUT and the MARCOING LINE within the Divisional Boundaries, in order to prepare the way for the 170th Inf. Bde. When the G.O.C. 170th Inf. Bde. has satisfied himself that the MARQUION line in F 20 and F 26 has been captured, and that our troops have passed beyond it, he will move his Brigade forward to the MARQUION LINE north of the inter-brigade boundary.
     O.C. A Coy will keep in close touch with G.O.C. 170th Inf. Bde. and will conform to the movements of the Brigade.
     In the event of a further advance O.C. A Coy will support the advancing infantry as the tactical situation demands - these supporting guns will be used with boldness.
     A Coy must be prepared to move forward of the MARQUION LINE at Zero plus 8 hours.

9. SUPPLIES. During the attack 2 days rations in addition to the emergency ration will be carried on the man.

10. CARRYING PARTIES. A Coy 2/5 L.N.L.R. (P) is attached to the Battn. they will be allotted as follows:-
     No. 1 Platoon to A Coy
     " 2 " " B "
     " 3 " " C "
     " 4 " " D "
They will move forward under the command of the O.C. Coys concerned.
4 men per Lewis Gun Section will accompany their platoons to the jumping off point, and will then return to 2nd Echelon, where they will be employed as a reserve carrying party and as guides. O.C. Coy will remain at 2nd Echelon.
     Stretcher bearers will accompany B & D Coys.
     Signallers will be attached to Battn. Signalling Officer.

11. **WATER.** 8 Petrol Tins per section will be carried forward by the gun teams.
A reserve water supply will be established on Sunken Road in E 30 a & c.
Empty petrol tins from B & D Coys will be filled from this point.
Section Officers are responsible that the utmost economy in the use of water is observed and that no other source of supply is used for drinking or cooking.

12. **S.A.A.** All possible ammunition will be carried forward.
A forward dump will be established in Sunken Road in E 30 a & c and a minimum of 50,000 rounds will be maintained there.
The R.S.M. will be in charge of reserve water and S.A.A. supply.

13. **SPARE GUNS.** A Gun and Spare parts store will be established at about E 29 a. 9.9. where damaged guns and spare parts will be sent for replacement or repair.
The Staff A.O.C. will be in charge.

14. **COMMUNICATION.** As soon as possible and advanced Battn Hd. Qrs. will be established at about E 28a. 9.9. (LYNX TRENCH) which will be in telephonic communication with Divn.
A guide will be at the junction of LYNX TRENCH and the main road. In the event of an advance beyond the final objective Adv B.H.Q. will move to the neighbourhood ANNEUX

15. **ADVANCED REPORT CENTRE.** The Signals Officer will arrnage for an A.R.C. at about F 19 c. 9.1. N.E. corner of ANNEUX.
He will establish Visual between Forward Coy Hd. Qrs. and Battn Hd. Qrs. and link up to the rear by telephone as soon as possible.

16. **RUNNERS.** (a) Mounted Orderlies. In addition to two troopers supplied by Divn. 6 mounted Orderlies will be detailed by B.T.O. to be employed between A.R.C. and Bn. H.Q.
They will report to the 2nd i/c at Z x 290 at the junction of LYNX TRENCH and the Main Road E 28 b. 4.5.
(b) Forward Coys will each keep one runner at A.R.C. Support and Reserve Coys will each keep one Runner at Advance Bn. H.Qrs.
8 Bn. Runners will be distributed between Bn. H.Qrs. & A.R.C.
(c) Pigeons. Pigeons if available will be kept at A.R.C.
In the event of 170th Inf. Bde. advancing A. Coy will pick these up.

17. **MEDICAL ARRANGEMENTS.** At each Inf. Bde H.Qrs. there will be a Bde. Bearer Medical Officer, who will arrange for the collection & evacuation of all wounded in the Bde. Area.
O.C. COYS must notify him if assistance is required.

18. **TRANSPORT.** (a) First Echelon. The B.T.O. will accompany the First Echelon Transport to E 29 b. & E 30 a. He will reconnoitre watering points & arrange for transport parks in this locality
He will report to Advanced Bn H.Qrs. when this has been done.

been done.
- (b) <u>2nd Echelon.</u>   2nd Echelon and details will be under the command of Major G.L.O. Grundy & will move up to positions in D 16 & 17 at an hour to be notified later. Major Grundy will establish communication with Divl Hd. Qrs & will be responsible for the supply of water, ammunition and rations to Coys and forward dumps.
  2nd in Commands of Companies will remain with 2nd Echelon.

19. <u>SYNCHRONISATION OF WATCHES.</u>   Watches will be synchronised at 7.0. p.m. to-day. Each Coy will send an Officer to report to the Adjutant at this hour.

ISSUED at 1.30. p.m. 26/9/18.

DISTRIBUTION

Copy No. 1.   57 Div. (G)
2.   170 Inf. Bde.
3.   171 " "
4.   172 " "
5.   A Coy.
6.   B "
7.   C "
8.   D "
9.   2 i/c
10. Major Grundy.
11. S.O.
12. B.T.O.
13. O.C. A Coy 2/5 L.N.L.R. (P)
14   File.
15/16   War Diary.

H.D. Oakeshott
Lieut
A/Adjt
57th Bn M.G.C.

ACCOUNT of 57th BATTN. M.G.C. OPERATIONS

from 27th to 30th SEPTR. 1918.

27th Sept.
1.45 a.m.
5.20 a.m.

The Battn. moved up from bivouac in NOREUIL to its assembly area via LAGNICOURT and track S. of QUEANT & PRONVILLE and at Zero hour was assembled as follows:-

"A" Coy D.15.d.   "B" Coy D.16.c.
"C" Coy D.21.b.   "D" Coy D.22.a.

Battn. Hd.Qrs. being established near Div. Hd.Qrs. at D.17.a.8.3. with 2nd Echelon behind at NOREUIL under Major G.L.O. GRUNDY.

6.15.a.m.

At 6.15 a.m. Coys were ordered to move forward to grid line D.18.c.0.0. D.20.c.0.0. D.30.c.0.0. and at 7 a.m.

7. a.m. when the order "57th Division Move" was given they were formed up about 200 short of this line.

From this point Coys were supposed to move forward independently in accordance with instructions laid down in "Warning Order" of 23rd and "Instruction No.1." of the 26th (Appendix 1).

Owing, however, to the attack on the 1st & 2nd objectives not being completed up to time and the bridges across the CANAL du NORD not being possible for transport, the Coys could not get forward and at 10 a.m. after several unsuccessful attempts to cross the Canal both on the main BAPAUME - CAMBRAI road and by the crossing in E.20.d. both of which places were being harassed by indirect M.G. fire, Coys were disposed as follows:-

10 a.m. "A" Coy in sunken road E.19.c.   "B","C", & "D" Coys in sunken road E.19.d.8.0. & E.19.d.9.7.

In moving forward "B" Coy was heavily shelled and sustained six casualties, and the O.C. "C" Coy Capt. O. Greenwood was wounded but remained at duty.

The situation at this time being very obscure Major J. Robin 2 i/c went forward in an endeavour to gain information.

Major Robin reported that at 10 a.m. the reserve Bde.

of the 63rd Divn were crossing the Canal and that enemy M.G. posts in LEOPARD TRENCH were only then being mopped up. He could find no trace of 171 & 172 Inf. Bdes and at 10.30 a.m. found the 1st Royal Munster Fusiliers under cover at No. 5 Lock in the CANAL du NORD. He then reconnoitred crossings over the Canal and found none passable for limbers.

11.45 a.m.   At 11.45 a.m. it was reported the troops of 172 Inf. Bds. were pushing forward to the HINDENBURG SUPPORT Line and orders were given to "B" & "D" Coys to transfer as many of their guns and as much ammunition as possible on to pack animals and to cross the Canal with all possible speed, the remainder of the guns to follow on limbers as soon as the tracks were made passable.

12.30 p.m.   By this time the Artillery had begun to move forward and the roads were so conjested that it was almost impossible to move in any direction. However by 2.30 p.m. the whole of "B" Coy and two sections each of "D" & "C" Coys were across the Canal.

At this hour the O.C. Battn. met the G.O's.C. 171 & 172 Inf. Bde. at Cross roads E.27.b. and remained in close touch with them for the remainder of the day.

3 p.m.   At 3 p.m. the 63rd Div. were reported to be still hung up at the Sugar Factory in E.29.a. and that the 171 & 172 Inf.Bdes. were advancing across the HINDENBURG SUPPORT Line. "B" Coy M.G.Battn supporting 171 on the left and two sections each of "C" & "D" Coys with 172 on the right. The remaining four sections of "C" & "D" which had by this time crossed the Canal were in support in E.27.b.

4 p.m.   About 4 p.m. the enemy were reported to be relinquishing their hold on GRAINCOURT & ANNEUX which our troops proceeded to occupy and at 6.30 M.G's were reported to be supporting the

infantry as follows:-

172 Inf. Bde. Area.

2 Sections (8 guns) "D" Coy on high ground S.E. of GRAINCOURT K.6.c.

2 Sections (8 guns) "D" Coy between ANNEUX and GRAINCOURT in E.30.c.

171 Inf. Bde. Area.

1 Section (4 guns) "B" Coy at E.23.b.3.7.

1 Section (4 guns) "B" Coy at E.22.d.9.9.

2 Sections (8 guns) in LYNX TRENCH E 22 a.

Support.

"C" Coy   16 guns   E.29.a.

Reserve.

"A" Coy   16 guns   E.21.c.

Battn. Hd.Qrs. was established at 6 p.m. at E 28 b.7.5.

7.15 p.m.   At 7.15 p.m. a enemy counter-attack was launched on ANNEUX from the S.E.   One Section of "D" Coy attempted to get into action against it but our own artillery barrage came down on top of them and they were forced to withdraw to sunken road in E.30.   2 men were wounded, 2 guns were put out of action by our artillery.

Sept. 28th.   On the morning of the 28th Septr. 171 & 172 Inf. Bdes. continued the attack, 171 Bde. on the left, with the object of clearing the ground between ANNEUX & FONTAINE and gaining touch with the Canadian Corps at the latter place.   172 Bde. on the right with the Sunken road E.28.d.6.5. to E.22.b.8.0. as their objective.   "B" Coy supporting 171 Bde. first took position as follows:- 1 Section in F.25.b. and 1 Section in

F.19.d. with two Sections in support W of ANNEUX. Then when the infantry advanced one Section of the ½ Coy in support pushed forward to positions in F.15.b. and one Section to F.22.c.   From these positions they brought indirect fire to bear on the MARCOING LINE in F.17 & 18. They remained in these positions for the remainder of the day.

On the right "D" Coy supporting 172 Inf.Bde. acted as follows:-

No. 1 Section advanced to N. of CANTAING and took up positions in F.28.a., No. 2 Section moving forward with 2/4th S.L.R. This Section was in touch with 2nd Division on right.   Guns first came into action in trench from L.3.a.50.15 to L.3.c.70.90.   Later, a request from O.C. 1st South Staffs for covering fire on high ground in A.26.a. & G.2.a. necessitated the guns being moved forward to L.4.b.& c.   From these positions harassing fire was directed on the retiring enemy. No. 3 Section came into action in F.21.b. and searched LA FOLIE WOOD with direct fire in support of 1st Royal Munster Fusiliers.

No. 4 Section after giving covering fire on CANTAING in the early stages of the attack advanced to positions F.28.a.

O.C. "A" Coy supporting 170 Inf.Bde. detailed No. 2 Section under 2nd Lt. F.Bell to accompany 2/5th K.O. (R.L) to assist them in their advance. The Section advanced behind the Battn. up to LA FOLIE WOOD. At this point the infantry were met with M.G.fire from behind the CHATEAU and the E edge of the wood. One of our guns was mounted and commenced searching the Wood with the result that after firing two belts the enemy's M.G. firing from that direction ceased.

2/Lt. Bell then went forward with 2 guns in support of "A" Coy 2/5 K.O.(R.L) who were advancing to the Canal Bank.

The infantry came under intense M.G.fire apparently from the
MARCOING LINE and Lt. Bell mounted his two guns at F.29.a.9.5.
covering the lock bridge.   He then went forward to
reconnoitre and on being told that an attempt was to be made
to cross the Canal he brought up his sub-section in support
and with four guns put a light barrage on the MARCOING LINE
and searched the road beyond.

      As soon as the infantry began crossing the Canal
he moved his section up to the Canal bank at F.29.b.5.4 and
from there brought direct fire to bear on the MARCOING LINE
and the crest beyond.

      The infantry were suffering heavy casualties and
were forced to fall back. 2/Lt. Bell then thinking he had
spotted the direction from which hostile fire was coming
endeavoured to mount a gun on top of a mound just South of the
lock bridge but his Sergeant and No. 1 were killed and he was
ordered to withdraw from that position.

    No. 3 Section of "A" Coy in support of 2/4 L.N.L.
advanced with the infantry and finally took up defensive
positions in F.22.b.5.4 without obtaining any targets.

    The dispositions of M.G's at midnight 28th/29th were
as follows:-

```
"B" Coy.   1 Section  F.25.b.
           1    "     F.19.d.
           1    "     F.15.b.
           1    "     F.22.c.

"D" Coy.   1    "     F.28.a.
           1    "     L.4.b.& c.
           1    "     F.21.b.
           1    "     F.28.b.

"A" Coy.   2 Sections & H.Q. F.20.b.
           1 Section  F.22.b.
           1    "     F.29.b.

"C" Coy    In Reserve
           4 Sections F.29.central.
```

5.

Sept. 29th.   On the morning of the 29th Septr. the 63rd Divn. went through the 57th Divn with the outskirts of CAMBRAI and high ground to the South as their objective. At 0415 hours the Drake Battn. formed a line between the Canal and River where they remained until the enemy were forced to withdraw from the MARCOING LINE owing to the 2nd Division on the right having penetrated it further South.

No. 2 Section of "A" Coy(2/Lt. Bell) opened fire on the enemy as they retired over the ridge to the East. 2/Lt. Bell then followed up the infantry and established his guns in positions in F.30.d.8.4. and F.30.c.8.8. In this position they were heavily bombed and machine gunned by hostile aeroplanes.

During the whole of the 28th & 29th 2/Lt. Bell handled his guns with much skill and dash and his Section was undoubtedly responsible for the deaths of many boches, both from the positions on the Canal Bank in F.30.b. and also from behind LA FOLIE WOOD.

The infantry state that this Section was instrumental in breaking up a counter-attack and also in preventing the enemy from getting round our flanks in LA FOLIE WOOD.

On the evening of the 29th 171 Inf.Bde. attacked on left of 63rd Divn.

O.C."B" Coy supporting 171 Bde. sent two sections across the Canal. These crossed the LOCK BRIDGE in F.29.b. at dusk and took up positions at F.24.c.7.3. covering the exits of PROVILLE. One section of "B" Coy moved forward to MARCOING LINE in F.18.c.c.6. and covered the Canal crossing in F.24.a. One section remaining in reserve in Sunken road West of LA FOLIE WOOD.

"D" Coy beyond some minor changes of gun positions

took no action on 29th.

Dispositions of M.G's at midnight 29th/30th were as follows:-

"A" Coy.   1 Section F.30.c.
            1   "   F.22.b.
            2 Sections (Support) F.20.b.

"B" Coy.   1 Section F.18.c.
            2 Sections F.24.c.
            1 Section (Support) F.22.d.

"D" Coy.   1 Section F.28 central.
            1   "   F.28.d.
            1   "   F.26.b.
            1   "   L.3.c.

"C" Coy   In reserve
            4 Sections E.29.central.

30th Sept.   172 Inf.Bde. received orders to cross the CANAL de l'ESCAUT with the object of clearing suburbs of CAMBRAI up to Line A 21,22,23,24,18 & 12. "D" Coy M.G. Battn was to assist in this operation acting as follows:-

One Section in support of 1st R.M.F. crossed the CANAL de l'ESCAUT to positions A 25 b. 20.covering high ground in A 26 a. & b.

One Section advancing with 2/4 S.L.R. came under heavy machine gun fire and took up position in A 20 c. from where one of its guns silenced an enemy machine gun firing from A.20.d. 0.8.

One section after assisting the 9th K.L.R. with covering fire took up position in A 26 a.

One section after firing 10 belts on to ground N.E. of PROVILLE from A.19.d.7.0. withdrew to position in F.30.a.8.4.

At 9 a.m. Septr. 30th Battn. Hd. Qrs. moved to F.15.d. 2.3.

On the evening of 39th Sept. A. Coy.

relieved "B" Coy and as it was considered likely that the enemy might counter-attack "C" Coy took up positions in MARCOING the main line of defence.

Dispositions at 2359 hours 30th Septr. were as follows:-

"B" Coy in Reserve.
    Coy H.Q. & 4 Sections F. 15b.4.0.

"A" Coy. Coy H.Q. F.22.d.5.2. with 4 guns.
        4 guns F.18.c.0.6.
        4 "   F.30.a.5.9.
        4 "   A.20.c.5.6.
        4 "   A.19.d.0.7.

"D" Coy. H.Q. F.28.a.8.2.
        2 guns A.26.a.9.3.
        2 "   A.26.b.15.25.
        2 "   A.20.c.5.5.
        2 "   A.20.c.8.4.
        4 "   F.30.b.& c. in reserve in trenches.
        1 gun at Bn. Hd.Qrs. 9th K.L.R. A.25.b.1.7.
        3 guns in trench A.19.a.7.9. to A.20.d.7.3.

"C" Coy.
        2 guns F.17.b. 5.6.
        2 "   F.17.a. 8.6.
        2 "   F.17.b. 9.2.
        2 "   F.17.b. 6.5.
        2 "   F.18.c. 2.9.
        2 "   F.18.c. 3.6.
        2 "   F.30.a. 5.9.

H.H.Oakeshott Capt for
Lieut Col
Comdg 57th Bn. MGC

Secret & Confidential

H.Q. 57th Div" (G)

Herewith War Diary
for October please

A.A.Oakeshott Capt.
Lieut. Col.
Commanding 57th Battn. M.G.C.

Army Form C. 2118.

357 Bn M.G. Corps
Vol 9

WAR DIARY
or
INTELLIGENCE SUMMARY.
(Erase heading not required.)

Instructions regarding War Diaries and Intelligence Summaries are contained in F. S. Regs., Part II. and the Staff Manual respectively. Title pages will be prepared in manuscript.

Place	Date	Hour	Summary of Events and Information	Remarks and references to Appendices
	Oct 1.		The operations from Octr. 1st - 9th are given in Appendix	App. I
	2.		Major C.H.B.Shepherd - Capt. G.V.Cox - Lieut E.W.Barber awarded the M.C.	
			146845 Pte. S. Wilson awarded M.M.	
			Major C.H.B.Shepherd wounded. Major G.L.O.Grundy appointed to command "D" Company.	
	3.		2/Lt. C.E.Johnson joined the Battn. from Base.	
			A draft of 30 reinforcements arrived.	
	4.		Lt. E.C.Jones and 13 O.R. reported missing in Z trench.	
	6.		Lt. J.H.P. Jones - H.S.Gent and 2/Lt. W. Jackson joined the Battn from Base.	
	9.		2/Lt. M.J.Gouley and a draft of 33 reinforcements joined from Base	
	13.		Capt. O.Greenwood and Lt. P.W.Dexter proceeded to Grantham for tour of duty	
			CASUALTIES 1st to 14th. Killed.	
			146734. Pte. Wicks J.C. D Coy. 6.-10-18.	
			71905. " Taylor J. C " 8-10-18.	
			58055 " Harwood F. C " Missing 4-10-18. Body found 9-10-18.	
			148140 " Priestman A.W. " " "	
			156089 " Trotter J.H. " " "	
			Died of Wounds.	
			140294 " Carson J. A " 1-10-18.	
			82706 " Sharpe G. " " 3-10-18.	
			158687 " Edmonds H. C " 2-10-18.	
			123446 " Nimmo J. D " 7-10-18.	
			163140 " Pitt G.W. A " 8-10-18.	
			10276 " Spencer R " 13-10-18.	

Lieut. Col.
Commanding 57th Battn. M.G.C.

Army Form C. 2118.

WAR DIARY
or
INTELLIGENCE SUMMARY.
(Erase heading not required.)

Instructions regarding War Diaries and Intelligence Summaries are contained in F. S. Regs., Part II. and the Staff Manual respectively. Title pages will be prepared in manuscript.

Place	Date	Hour	Summary of Events and Information	Remarks and references to Appendices
			Wounded.	
			Major C.H.B.Shepherd, M.C. D Coy 1-10-18.	
			15429 Pte. Woods G. C " "	
			37345 Sgt. Derrick B. C " "	
			29471 Pte. Davies W. C " "	
			39563 " Elphinstone G.N. C " "	
			116117 " Andrews W. C 4-10-18.	
			112779 L/C Newlands T.G. C " "	
			46239 Pte Duggan L. C " "	
			157913 " Talbot G. C " "	
			59026 " Cox E.G. C " "	
			152434 " McGuinness W. D 5-10-18.	
			26823 " Roberts J.A. D " "	
			42712 " Roe M. D " "	
			146075 " Dance F. D " "	
			64909 L/C Richards A.A. D 6-10-18	
			64897 Pte Adamson C D " "	
			145096 " Stafford T B " "	
			60620 Cpl Grimshaw H B 7-10-18 at duty	
			31026 Pte Mason A. B " "	
			122356 L/C Wilkinson J.H. D " "	
			122427 Pte Maidwell G.H. D " "	
			63912 " Quick G. D " "	
			152833 " Osborne W. D " "	
			65376 " Groutage W. D 8-10-18	
			58878 " Morrell S. C " "	
			58946 Cpl Walker J. C " "	
			35392 Sgt.Scott J. A " "	
			159277 Pte Poore R. A " "	
			159532 " Fear E. A " "	
			67180 " Pye A. A " "	
			136176 " Powlesland S.J. C " "	
			140276 " Spencer R. A " "	
				67225 L/C McCallem H. A Coy 1-10-18
				126253 Pte Elliott S.F. A Coy 1-10-18
				129683 " McIntyre M A " "
				146892 " Shea F.G. D " "

.... Lieut. Col.
Commanding 57th Battn. M.G.C.

Army Form C. 2118.

WAR DIARY
or
INTELLIGENCE SUMMARY.
(Erase heading not required.)

Place	Date	Hour	Summary of Events and Information	Remarks and references to Appendices
Map Sheets 57C 44B Béthune Coulomb 36.				
			Wounded. 53938. Sgt Mottram S.C. B Coy 8-10-18 144456 Pte Wiseman D. " " " Missing. Lt. E.C.Jones C Coy. 4-10-18. 58269 Sgt. Bullas F. " " 102262 L/C Evans W. " " 158678 Pte. Excell F.W. " " 54786 " Fielden E.B. " " 64637 " Wobley A. " " 158885 " Hough T. " " 148142 " Dean E. " " 155198 " Swift J. " " 58059 " Starkie W. " " 146924 " Hicks J.H. " "	APP. II
MOEUVRES.	Oct 10		On the 10th the Battn. marched from Fontaine Notre Dame to bivouac in D.29.	
	" 11		The Battn. rested. The bulk of the Transport under Capt. G.V.Cox, M.C. moved off at 10.45 hours to new area by road.	
	" 12		On the afternoon of the 12th the Battn personnel marched to HERMIES and entrained for FOUQUEREUIL arriving at 0420 hours, the remaining portions of the transport travelling by 2 separate trains under 2/Lt. F. Houghton & Lt. R. Harris respectively.	
FOUQUEREUIL BRAQUEMONT.	" 13		On arrival at FOUQUEREUIL xxxxxxxx the Battn. marched to BRAQUEMONT (NOEUX LES MINES) arriving at 0700 hours. On arrival orders were received that the Battn would move to LAVENTIE area the next day.	
PONT RIQUEUL BOUT DEVILLE FROMELLES.	" 14		On the 14th the Battn less D.Coy moved to LAVENTIE area to relieve 47th Division.	

[signature] Lieut. Col.
Commanding 57th Battn. M.G.C.

Army Form C. 2118.

WAR DIARY
or
INTELLIGENCE SUMMARY.
(Erase heading not required.)

Instructions regarding War Diaries and Intelligence Summaries are contained in F. S. Regs., Part II. and the Staff Manual respectively. Title pages will be prepared in manuscript.

Place	Date	Hour	Summary of Events and Information	Remarks and references to Appendices
Sheet 36	Oct. 15th		A Coy to BOUT DEVILLE) by route March. C " to PONT RIQUEUL) B " by Bus and march to FROMELLES Battn. Hd. Qrs. by March to PONT RIQUEUL D Coy remained at BRAQUEMONT.	App II App III App IV
PONT RIQUEUL. FROMELLES.			Owing to lessening resistance on the part of the enemy the right Brigade was pushed forward and the relief of 47th Divn was postponed for 24 hours. A Coy moved up to FROMELLES and then forward to CHATEAU de FLANDRES O.15.d. central under orders of 142 Bde (47th Divn) Lt. NEALE and 2nd Lt. NAYLER with 30 O.R. reinforcements joined the Battn. 2nd Lt. W. ARCHIBALD rejoined from Hospital. Two motor lorries were sent back to MONCHIET for stores, one broke down and failed to arrive.	
PONT RIQUEUL	16th		Bn. Hd. Qrs. remained at PONT RIQUEUL A Coy CHATEAU de FLANDRES. B " moved up to RADINGHEM C " PONT RIQUEUL in reserve. D " LE MAISNIL.	
FROMELLES	17th		Bn. Hd. Qrs. moved forward to FROMELLES & 2nd Echelon to WANGERIE A Coy at FROMELLES B " SEQUEDIN C " in reserve at AUBERS. D " CANTELEU.	

(signed) .... Lieut. Col.
Commanding 57th Battn. M.G.C.

Army Form C. 2118.

WAR DIARY
or
INTELLIGENCE SUMMARY.
(Erase heading not required.)

Instructions regarding War Diaries and Intelligence Summaries are contained in F.S. Regs., Part II. and the Staff Manual respectively. Title pages will be prepared in manuscript.

Place	Date	Hour	Summary of Events and Information	Remarks and references to Appendices
Sheet 36. N. ENGLOS.	Oct. 18th		Battn. Hd. Qrs. moved forward to ENGLOS. A Coy to Divisional Reserve at FIN de la GUERRE. B " with 172 at SEQUEDIN. C " relieved A Coy and moved to CANTELEU with 170 Bde. D " with 171 Bde. at HELLEMMES. 2nd Lieuts. H.E.T. Scowsoill, T.R. Binks and 35 O.R. joined from Base.	
Pt RONCHIN (LILLE)	19th.		Battn. Hd. Qrs. moved forward to Pt. RONCHIN Q.28.a.9.5. A Coy Pt. RONCHIN Q.21.c.80.95. B " with 172 Bde. at SEQUEDIN. C " " 170 " " HELLEMMES. D " - " 171 " " ASCQ. The 2nd Echelon moved up during the afternoon to Pt. RONCHIN.	
	20th		Bn. Hd. Qrs. no change. A Coy to CANTELEU J.36.c.60.15. B " " WILLEMS N.11.b.3.3. C " " D " " FME DE MARAIS N.9.a.55.50. A lorry was sent back to MONCHIET & remainder of Stores brought to PT. RONCHIN & a dump formed in BISCUIT FACTORY. Packs and blankets issued to Coys.	
WILLEMS (LE DARU)	21st		Bn. Hd. Qrs. moved forward to LE DARU M.17.b.04. A Coy ASCQ R.16.b.5.6. B " ASCQ R.11.c.2.2. C " TEMPLEUVE H.33.a.2.6. D " FME LE MARAIS N.9.a.55.50.	

.... Lieut. Col.
Commanding 57th Battn. M.G.C.

Army Form C. 2118.

WAR DIARY
or
INTELLIGENCE SUMMARY.
(Erase heading not required.)

Instructions regarding War Diaries and Intelligence Summaries are contained in F. S. Regs., Part II. and the Staff Manual respectively. Title pages will be prepared in manuscript.

Place	Date	Hour	Summary of Events and Information	Remarks and references to Appendices
Sheet 37	Oct. 22nd		The enemy holding the line of CANAL de L'ESCAUT with MT.AUBERT in rear - the advance was checked	
LE DARU			B Coy moved from ASCQ to LE DARU M.17.b.0.7.	
	23rd		Remainder no change.	
			No change.	
			Lieut. F.W.Wilkinson (1st Glos.) attached as Transport Officer proceeded to U.K. to report to Air Ministry.	App V
	24th		B Coy relieved D Coy in the line. Coy Hd.Qrs. Fms. LE MARAIS	
			Dispositions - Bn.Hd.Qrs. M.17.b.0.4. A Coy in reserve R.16.b.5.6. B " with 172 Bde. N.9.a.5.0. C " " 170 " H.33.a.2.6. D " " 171 " M.17.b.0.7.	
			3 Driver reinforcements reported from Base.	
	25th		No change.	
			Positions reconnoitred for main defensive line	
	26th		A Coy moved up from ASCQ to (LE DARU) WILLEMS in order to be closer to Battn.Hd.Qrs.	
			1 Coy 2/5 L.N.L.R. (Pioneers) detailed to act as carriers to 2 forward Companies in case of enemy withdrawal. Allotted 2 platoons to each Coy.	
			2nd Lt. D.J.Phillips admitted to Hospital.	

A. Nall Neebh............. Lieut. Col
Commanding 57th Battn. M.G.C.

Army Form C. 2118.

WAR DIARY
or
INTELLIGENCE SUMMARY.
(Erase heading not required).

Place	Date	Hour	Summary of Events and Information	Remarks and references to Appendices
Sheet 37.	Oct. 27th		No change.	
	28th		A Coy moved 3 sections in support forward, 2 going to C Coys H.Q. & reconnoitring positions for 4 guns about O.6.b.7.8. - 4 guns H.30.d.9.3. 1 going to B.Coys Hd.Qrs. and reconnoitring positions for 4 guns about O.13.a. 7.9. These sections coming under the tactical command of O.C's Left & Right groups respectively	App VI App VII
			Dispositions Bn.Hd.Qrs. M.17.b.0.4.	
			A Coy M.11.b.7.9.	
			B " N. 9.a.5.0.	
			C " A.33.a. 2.6.	
			D " M.17.b.0.7.	
LE DARU	29th		No change.	
			CASUALTIES. 15th to 31st Octr.	
			Killed.	
			138364. Pte. Kerr J. D Coy. 23-10-18.	
			Wounded.	
			106870 Pte Stokes B.S. C Coy 22-10-18.	
			133809 " Mann S.V. C " " at duty.	
			45087. Sgt. Newton H.W. C " 25-10-18 at duty.	
			15067 L/C Bune A. C " 26-10-18 at duty.	
			58052 Pte Catterall C.C C " 26-10-18	
			157275 " Cook W.H. C " 22-10-18	
			170727 " Batten E. C " 22-10-18	
			156548 " Ryley G. C " 30-10-18	
			14303 " Johnson R. C " "	

R. Olah Siehl
Lieut. Col.
Commanding 57th Battn. M.G.C.

Army Form C. 2118.

WAR DIARY
or
INTELLIGENCE SUMMARY

(Erase heading not required.)

Instructions regarding War Diaries and Intelligence Summaries are contained in F. S. Regs., Part II. and the Staff Manual respectively. Title Pages will be prepared in manuscript.

Place	Date	Hour	Summary of Events and Information	Remarks and references to Appendices
Sheet 36	Octr. 30th		No. change.	
MONS EN BAROEUL	31st		"D" Coy relieved by "B" Coy 47th Battn. M.G.C. "D" Coy moved to billets at MONS en BAROEUL.	

P. Neil Siehl
Lieut. Col.
Commanding 57th Battn. M.G.C.

MAP REF.
Sheet 57c 1/40000

App I

57th BATTN. M.G.C.

ACCOUNT of OPERATIONS from 1st Octr. to 9th Octr. 1918.

On the morning of Octr. 1st the Divisional boundary was re-adjusted so that the southern boundary ran through F.24.Central A.21.Central. This necessitated 52nd Bn. taking over gun positions of "D" Coy which was withdrawn and in its turn relieved "C" Coy in the MARCOING LINE.

"C" Coy was then withdrawn into support two sections being placed under the tactical control of O.C. "A" Coy who was supporting 170 Inf. Bde. on the right.

At 1330 hours 170th Inf. Bde. received orders to attack trench running from A 15 c.6.5. to A,22,a.0.0. in co-operation with 52nd Divn on right whose objective was FAUBOURG DE PARIS.

57th Bn.M.G.C. had orders to assist attack by means of a overhead fire in conjunction with artillery barrage and to send forward 2 Sections to help in the consolidation of the objective when gained.

"A" Coy therefore brought eight guns to bear on houses in A.16.c.& d. and fired at "medium" rate from Zero to Zero x 60.

O.C. "C" Coy received orders to send two sections forward to assist in the consolidation. One section (NO.2) received orders to advance in rear of infantry by way of Proville to take up positions to protect right flank of the objective; one section (No.3) to support left flank.

The attack failed and O.C. No.2 Section lost touch with the attacking infantry as they had gone too far to the left. In endeavouring to gain touch he advanced up sunken road through A.20.b. and on reaching the road junction in A.21.a. was fired on by enemy M.G's. The section then withdrew leaving three guns behind and took up defensive position in trench A.20.c.5.8.

No. 3 Section being unable to advance took up position in A.19.b.31, one gun being sent forward to assist No. 2 Section.

On the left of the main attack "C" Coy 2/4 L.N.L. carried out a minor operation against Z trench in A.15.a.& c. and reached their objective. At 2000 hours the infantry asked for m.g. assistance to protect their right flank.

One sub-section "C" Coy was detailed for this and a guide for them was provided by O.C. 2/4 L.N.L. The sub-section officer received orders to take up a position some way in rear of the objective on the bank of the ESCAUT River. Whether he lost his way in the dark, or whether he could not find a suitable position in rear is not known. However he took his sub-section right into the captured trench, was subsequently surrounded with the remainder of the garrison and with the exception of two runners who returned to Bn. H.Q. on the morning of Octr. 2nd none of the sub-section were again seen.

Dispositions on night of Octr. 1st/2nd were as follows:-

"A" Coy. H.Q. F.22.d.5.2.
          4 guns F.3.a.5.9.
            "   A.20.c.5.6.
            "   A.19.d.0.7.
            "   F.18.c.0.8.

"C" Coy. H.Q. F.21.d.9.6.
          2 guns A.15.b.0.0.
          2 "   A.20.d.5.8.
          4 "   A.19.b.3.1
          6 "   F.2.d.9.6.

"B" Coy. Reserve. FONTAINE.

"D" Coy. H.Q. F.22.d.7.2. & 4 guns.
          4 guns F.17.b.7.3.
          2 "   F.11.c.9.0.
          2 "   F.17.b.3.4.
          2 "   F.18.c.2.9.
          2 "   F.18.c.0.5.

Oct. 2nd.   On Octr. 2nd no offensive operations took place. Guns were moved forward to positions in PROVILLE and on the Aerodrome N. of the Canal.

In the evening "C" Coy made an attempt to regain guns

lost the previous night but without success.

Dispositions at 2389 hours as follows:-

"A" Coy. H.Q.   F.22.b.5.2.
          2 guns A.13.d.3.3.
          2 "   A. 8.c.1.3.
          4 "   F.30.a.5.9.
          4 "   A.20.c.5.6.
          4 "   A.20.b.4.2.

"C" Coy. Support.
          H.Q.   F.21.d.9.6.
          11 guns F.21.d.9.6.
          2 "   A.15.b.0.0.

"D" Coy. Unchanged.

"B" Coy. Reserve FONTAINE.

Oct. 3rd.   "A" Coy withdrew into reserve at F.21.b. being relieved by "C" Coy in right Bde. sector and by "B" Coy in left Bde. sector.

Dispositions at 2359 hours as follows:-

"A" Coy   Reserve. F.21.b.

"B" Coy   H.Q.& 2 sections FONTAINE.
          2 guns A.13.b.9.2.
          2 "   A.14.b.2.7.
          2 "   A.13.d.6.4.
          2 "   A. 8.c.1.3.

"C" Coy   H.Q. & 2 guns F.22.b.4.4.
          2 guns A.13.d.9.7.
          2 "   A. 8.c.1.3.
          4 "   A.20.b.5.2.
          4 "   A.19.d.0.6.
          4 "   A.14.c.8.8.

"D" Coy. Unchanged.

Oct. 4th.   "A" Coy   In reserve   ANNEUX.

"B" Coy   Unchanged.

"C" Coy. H.Q & 2 guns F.22.b.4.4.
          2 guns from A.13.d.9.7. to A.20.b.6.8. &
                       thence to A.14.c.8.8.
          2 guns from A.8.c.1.3. to A.14.c.3.0. &
                       thence to A.14.c.2.8.
          2 "   A.14.c.2.5.
          4 "   A.20.b.5.2.
          4 "   A.19.a.0.6.

"D" Coy   unchanged.

Oct. 5th.   "B" Coy relieved "D" Coy in MARCOING LINE.

Dispositions at 1800 hours:-

"A" Coy   Unchanged.

"B" Coy   relieved "D" Coy. Headqrs remained FONTAINE
    1 Section   F.18.c.0.7.
    2 guns   F.17.b.0.5.
    2 "   F.11.c.8.0.
    2 "   A.14.b.2.7.
    2 "   A.13.b.9.2.
    2 "   A.13.d.6.4.
    2 "   A 8.c.1.3.

"C" Coy 2 guns from A.14.c.2.5. to A.19.b.9.2.
    remainder unchanged.

"D" Coy in reserve FONTAINE.

Oct 6th.   "A" Coy   unchanged

"B" Coy   2 guns from A.13.d.6.4. took over from
    52nd Bn. at F.18.c.4.6.

"C" Coy   2 guns from A.14.c.2.5. & A.14.c.3.0.
    took over from 52nd Bn. at F.17.b.8.3.

"D" Coy.   Coy H.Q. & 4 guns FONTAINE.
    4 guns to F.28.a.)   To relieve
    4   "   F.29.b.)   Coy of
    4   "   F.22.b.)   52nd Bn.

The Support Coy of 52nd Bn.M.G.C. guarding the bridges over the CANAL de l'ESCAUT was relieved by "D" Coy.

The two Coys of 52nd Bn.M.G.C. in the forward area passed under the control of O.C. 57th Bn. M.G.C. They were disposed as follows:-

    4 guns   A.27.c.10.05.
    2 guns   A.26.d.60.00
    2 "   A.26.b.7.7.
    2 "   A.20.d.2.1.
    4 "   A.26.a.7.6.
    2 "   A.26.c.5.9.
    4 "   A.25.d.6.9.
    4 "   A.25.d.9.1.
    8 "   Support MARCOING LINE.

Oct. 7th. "A" Coy. Two sections sent forward ready to support attack on morning of 8th in co-operation with 2/4 L.N.L. Regt. 2 Sections in reserve at FONTAINE.

"B" Coy. 2 guns from F.18.c.4.6. moved to BUTTE de TIR at A.13.b.9.2. 4 guns also at this position ready to shoot along road A.22.a.1.0. to A.22.d.3.6.

"C" Coy   unchanged.

"D" Coy   "

Oct. 8th On the morning of the 8th the 63rd Division attacked with the high ground N.E. of NIERGNIES as their objective. At the same time 170th Bde. formed a defensive flank along trench line G.4.b.6.6. to A.27.d.2.0. Zero hour was at 0430 hours.

To assist the attack Two sections of "A" Coy were detailed to assist 170 Inf. Bde. in the consolidation of their objective, 2 sections remaining in reserve at FONTAINE.

During the attack 57th & 52nd M.G.Bns. supported the infantry with overhead fire as under.

57th Bn.M.G.C.
```
 4 Guns firing on road A.22.c.05.85. to
                       A.22.a.15.15.
 4   "     "    "   "  junction A.22.c.8.8.
 4   "     Fbg.de Paris A.27.b.7.9. to
                       A.21.d.80.35.
 2   "                 Road A.28.b.15.80 to
                       A.22.d.2.2.
 4   "                 Trench A.28.a.& b.
```
52nd Bn.M.G.C.
16 guns distributed over sunken road in A.28.c. Railway A.28.d.& A.23.c. Cross Roads A.22.d.

All these guns fired at slow rate of 1 belt every 4 mins. from Z to Z x 20 and at rate of 1 belt per 10 mins. from Zero x 20 to Zero x 180.

About 1200 hours the infantry reported that they were being troubled by m.g. fire from trench in A.28.a.& b. 4 guns therefore kept up intermittent bursts on this trench for two hours.

In all about 90,000 rounds were fired by 57th B_n.M.G.C.

The two sections of "A" Coy detailed to assist in consolidation moved up behind the infantry. One section took up positions 2 guns in G.3.b.2.8. and 2 guns G.3.b.3.7. from where they successfully engaged m.g's. in A.28a. & A.27.b. with direct fire. The other section placing 2 guns in G.4.c.5.4. and 2 guns in G.4.a.6.3.

The two sections in reserve in FONTAINE were moved forward to give depth to the defence of captured position and took up positions as follows:-

    2 guns G.3.b.9.4. and 2 guns in G.4.d.0.5.

One section remained in reserve in the Quarry at G.8.b.7.1.

On the evening of Octr. 8th 52nd M.G.Bn. withdrew one Coy from forward area into support leaving guns as under:-

    2 guns A.27.b.1.0.
    2 "   A.26.a.7.0.
    2 "   A.26.b.8.8.
    2 "   A.26.a.7.7.
    2 "   A.25.d.6.9.
    2 "   A.25.d.9.1.
    4 guns in support MARCOING LINE.

Oct. 9th.   During the night 8th/9th the enemy evacuated CAMBRAI.

At 1800 hours the Battn. was ordered to concentrate and all guns were withdrawn to the FONTAINE area.

REMARKS.

COMMUNICATIONS.

Much difficulty was experienced by Bn.H.Q. in keeping in touch with Coys during the early stages of the operations especially on Z day. This was partly due to the fact that the initial attack did not progress according to programme and therefore the Companies were unable to establish their headquartrs in the localities laid down and partly to the fact that Company Commanders themselves did not keep in close touch with Bde. H.Q.

In operations such as those of Sept. 27th & subsequent days it is impossible for a M.G.Bn. to lay and maintain its own lines of communication and it must rely on the Divisional lines to Brigades for communication with Coys. This was not generally realized by Coy Commanders who attempted to communicate direct with Bn.H.Q. and did not keep Bde. H.Q. informed of their location. The two mounted orderlies of the 6th D.G's attached to the Bn. were of the greatest service but they were not sufficient to cope with the work.

No. 5 Signal Section attached to the Bn. H.Q. worked well & visual signalling stations established by them proved of great value on Septr. 28th & 29th.

CARRYING PARTIES.

The Coy of Pioneers attached to the Bn. for the operations were of the very greatest value. Without their help it would have been found very difficult to keep as many guns as we did in action. Their help enabled guns to be man-handled over greater distances than would have been possible otherwise, thereby greatly reducing the number of casualties to animals which in spite of that was considerable.

PACK TRANSPORT.

On Septr. 29th much difficulty was caused in crossing the CANAL DU NORD owing to the lack of training of the personnel of the Bn. Apart from casualties due to enemy fire no animals were evacuated sick and their condition was maintained under very adverse circumstances.

CASUALTIES.

Casualties during the period Sept. 27th to Oct. 9th were as follows:-

OFFICERS.

Killed.
2/Lt. P.L.Hedgcock   D.Coy.   30-9-18.
"   W. Pearson.   B "   29-9-18.

Wounded.
Capt. O. Greenwood   C "   27-9-18 at duty.
Major C.H.B.Shepherd
                M.C. D "   1-10-18.
2/Lt. W. Clark   D "   30-9-18. (Accidental)

Missing.
Lieut. E.C.Jones   A "   4-10-18.

OTHER RANKS.

Killed 11
Wounded 69
Died of Wds. 7
Missing 11

ANIMALS.

	R.	L.D.M.
Killed.	5	22.
Wounded	1.	13.
Missing	-	4.

_____ Lieut. Col.
Commanding 27th Battn. M.G.C.

SECRET.   Copy No. 12

Ref. Map 36 N.W. 1/20,000   13/10/18.
        36 S.W.

    BETHUNE   1/40,000.

               57th BATTN. M.G.C. WARNING ORDER.

1.   From midnight 13th/14th Octr. 57th Division (less Artillery)
will come under orders of XI Corps and will relieve 47th Division
in the right Divisional Sector of XI Corps front by 0600 hours
17th October.

2.   All defence instructions, maps of the Divisional Sector,
air photographs, will be handed over by 47th Division on relief.

3.   Command of right Divisional Sector will pass to G.O.C.
57th Division at 1800 hours on 16th October, at which hour Divisional
Hd. Qrs. will close at L'EPINETTE and open at RIEZ - BAILLEUL.

4.   Machine Guns will act as follows:-
        (a) "B" Coy 57th Battn. M.G.C. will relieve the Coy holding the
            right Brigade section on the night 15th/16th

        (b) "D" Coy 57th Battn. M.G.C. will relieve the Coy holding
            the left Brigade section on the night 16th/17th.

        (c) "A" Coy will be in support.

        (d) "C" Coy will be in reserve.

5.   (a) "B" Coy will embuss with 172 Inf. Bde. Group at
embussing point E 29 c. 5.5. at about 0800 hours on the 14th inst.
        to proceed to support area 47th Division (FROMELLES - le -
        MAISNIL) Route BETHUNE - RICHEBOURG L'AVOUE - PONT LOGY
        thence by M. 34b. 3.6. - PIETRE - N 31 d. 1.1. - AUBERS.

        (b) "B" Coys transport will proceed by march route with 172
            Inf. Bde. Group as above not to pass W 29 c.5.5. before
            1000 hours - move to be completed by 1800.

        (c) A haversack ration will be carried. Dinners will be
            cooked with transport en route and eaten on arrival.

6.   Battn. Hd. Qrs. - "A" & "C" Coys will be attached to 170 Inf.
Bde. Group and will proceed to FOSSE - BOUT DEVILLE area by march
route on 14th inst. via BETHUNE - LOCON.
        Probable time of start 0930 hours.
        Dinners will be eaten on the road.

7.   (a) "D" Coy will embuss at E 19 b.3.0. with 171 Inf. Bde.
            group on 15th inst. at about 0800 hours to PONT LOGY & thence
            by march route to FROMELLES - le - MAISNIL area as para.5.(a).

        (b) "D" Coys transport will proceed by march route as para.
            5 (b) not to pass starting point K.19.b.3.0. before 1000 hours-
            march to be completed by 1800 hours.

        (c) A haversack ration will be carried and dinners cooked
            with transport en route and eaten on arrival.

8. One water cart will be attached to each Company.

9. Stores that cannot possibly be carried will be dumped at Q.M. Stores before units move off and will be carried on Motor lorry on 15th inst.

10. The following minimum distance will be maintained between units on the march:-
    Between Companies, and units, their transport)
    and transport of units when brigaded   ) 100 yards
    Between Battalions   500   "

11. ACKNOWLEDGE.

12. Further orders will be issued later.

                                        H.R.Oakeshott, **Capt & Adjt.**
                                           57th Battn.M.G.C.

Issued at 2100 hours.

Distribution-

Copy No. 1. 57th Divn (G)
       2. 170 Inf.Bde.
       3. 171 "   "
       4. 172 "   "
       5. A Coy
       6   B "
       7. C "
       8. D "
       9. Q.M.
      10. B.T.O.
      11. Sig. Officer
   12/13. War Diary.
      14   File.

SECRET.

Ref. Map.   BETHUNE (Combined) 1/40,000.   Copy No. 5
            36 S.W.   1/20,000.
                                                14/10/18.

57th BATTN. M.G.C. OPERATION ORDER No. 41.

1. 57th Battn. M.G.C. will relieve 47th Battn. M.G.C. on the 14th 15th & 16th inst. Relief to be completed by 0600 hours on the 17th.

2. Relief will be carried out as follows:-

   (a) Octr. 14th.   "B" Coy 57th Bn. will relieve "A" Coy 47th Bn. in reserve area. Coy Hd.Qrs. N.27.a.8.4.
   (b) Octr. 15th.   Morning. "A" Coy 57th Bn. will relieve "D" Coy 47th Bn. in support. Coy Hd.Qrs. N.16.d.8.8.
   (c)   "   "   Afternoon. "D" Coy 57th Bn. will relieve "B" Coy 57th Bn. in reserve area. Coy Hd.Qrs. N.27.a.8.4.
   (d) Night 15th/16th. "B" Coy 57th Bn. will relieve "C" Coy 47th Bn. in the Right Sector. Coy Hd.Qrs. FROMELLES CHATEAU N.23.c.15.40.
   (e) Octr. 16th.   Afternoon. "C" Coy 57th Bn. will relieve "D" Coy 57th Bn. in reserve area. Coy Hd.Qrs. N.27.a.8.4.
   (f) Night 16th/17th. "D" Coy 57th Bn. will relieve "B" Coy 47th Bn. in the Left Sector. Coy Hd.Qrs. O.13.c.85.65.

3. O.C.Coys 57th Bn. will get into touch with O.C.Coys 47th Bn. whom they are relieving. All details of relief will be arranged between O.C.Coys concerned.

4. Completion of each relief will be reported to 57th Bn. Hd. Qrs. by code word "HOPE" stating time & casualties. O.C.Coys will personally report to Bdes. in whose sectors they are on completion of relief.

5. TRANSPORT. Fighting Limbers & Cookers will be kept at Coy. Hd. Qrs. remainder of Transport will be at Bn. 2nd Echelon in WANGERIE M.17.b.8.6.

6. SOFT CAPS. Service caps will be packed in sand bags by gun teams and stored in Coy Q.M.Stores. No soft caps will be taken into the line.

7. REPORTS. Intelligence reports will be made out to cover the period from 0600 hours to 0600 hours and will be rendered daily to reach Bn.Hd.Qrs. by 1000 hours.

8. All maps aeroplane photographs etc. will be taken over by ingoing Coys.

9. Consolidated list of maps, trench stores, etc. will be sent in to Bn.Hd.Qrs. within 12 hours of completion of relief.

10.   Battn. Hd. Qrs. will close at R.9.b.8.5. and open at
SIEN BAILLEUL M.7.b.3.0. at 1500 hours on the 15th. Until this
hour communication with 57th Battn. will be through 47th Battn.
Location of Coys on various dates will be in accordance with
attached list.

11.   ACKNOWLEDGE Coys only.

                                                      H.A.Oakeshott.   Capt. & Adjt.
                                                        57th Battn. M.G.C.

Issued at 1830 hours 14/10/18.

Distribution-

    Copy No. 1 57th Divn (G)
             2 170 Inf. Bde.
             3 171 "   "
             4 172 "   "
             5 47th Bn. M.G.C.
             6 200 Bn. M.G.C.
             7 74th Bn. M.G.C.
             8 A Coy
             9 B "
           10 C "
           11 D "
           12 Q.M.
           13 M.O.
           14 R.T.O.
     15/16 War Diary.
           17 File.

SECRET.   16/10/18.

57th BATTN. M.G.C.

Reference OPERATION ORDER No. 41 dated 14/10/18.-

1. Relief is postponed for 24 hours.

2. Until relief is complete "A", "B", & "D" Coys will be under orders of O.C. 47th Battn. M.G.C.

3. "B" Coy 57th Battn. M.G.C. will remain with 172 Inf. Bde. and relieve "B" Coy 47th Battn. M.G.C. in the Left Section under orders of O.C. 47th Battn. M.G.C.

4. "D" Coy 57th Battn. M.G.C. will remain with 171 Inf. Bde. and will relieve "C" Coy 47th Battn. in the Right Section under orders of O.C. 47th Battn. M.G.C.

5. "A" Coy 57th Battn. M.G.C. will remain at the disposal of G.O.C. 142nd Inf. Bde. under orders of O.C. 47th Bn.M.G.C.

6. Until 57th Divn take over, all reports and dispositions of "A", "B" & "D" Coys 57th Battn. M.G.C. will be sent to O.C. 47th Battn. M.G.C.

7. Battn. Hd. Qrs. 57th Battn. M.G.C. will close at PONT RIQUEUL at 1500 hours on the 17th and open at FROMELLES N.22.b.8.7. at the same hour.

8. Coys 57th Battn. M.G.C. will acknowledge.

H.W.Onkeshott
Capt. & Adjt.
57th Battn. M.G.C.

To all recipients of 57th Battn. M.G.C.
Operation Order No. 41. dated 14/10/18.

Ref. Map Sheet 37 1/40,000. Copy No. 7.

24/10/18.

57th BATTN. M.G.C. OPERATION ORDER No. 42.

1. 172nd Inf.Bde. and the 505th Field Coy R.E. will relieve 171st Inf.Bde. and 421st Field Coy R.E. in the Right Section of Divisional Front on the night 24th/25th October.

2. "B" Coy 57th Battn.M.G.C. will relieve "D" Coy 57th Battn. M.G.C. on the 24th.

3. All arrangements for relief will be made direct between Coys concerned.

Completion of relief will be reported to this Office and to Bdes. concerned.

4. On relief "D" Coy will be in Divisional reserve and will take over "B" Coys billets in WILLEMS area.

(Sd) H.A.Oakeshott. Capt & Adjt.
57th Battn.M.G.C.

Issued at 1045 hours.

Distribution-

Copy No. 1 57th Division (G)
    2. 171 Inf.Bde.
    3. 172 "   "
    4. "B" Coy.
    5. "D" "
    6/7 War Diary.
    8 File.

App VI

SECRET.

57th BATTN. M.G.C.
INSTRUCTIONS FOR THE DEFENCE.

DEFENCE.

1. The Divisional Sector extends from O.16.a.0.0. to O.26.b.0.0.

2. The Sector is held by two Brigades in depth each on a one Battalion front.

   Boundary between Brigades - N.3.central & thence due East.

3. The defensive organisation consists of :-

   (a) Outpost System.

      The main line of resistance of this system runs generally along the TOURNAI - PONT A CHIN Road to PONT A CHIN and thence along Canal Bank.
      Should any part of this line be lost, it will be at once regained by counter-attack.
      The Right Brigade will be prepared to form a defensive flank running South of PROYENNES to connect with the Outpost main line of resistance of the Division on our right at O.13.c.5.0. should the forward posts of that Division be driven back.
      On the left the main line of resistance connects with that of the Division on our left at I.26.a.5.0.

   (b) Second System.

      The main line of resistance of this System runs through O.13.b.5.0. - O.13.b.1.8. - O.7.c.central - O.7.a. central - O.1.c.central and thence just East of FOURCROIX and just East of RUMES.
      This line will connect with the outpost line of resistance of the Division on our right at O.13.a.5.0.
      The Left Brigade will be prepared in the event of the Outpost Line of Resistance being temporarily lost to man a switch line running from East of RUMES past the Southern edge of RAMBONIES-CHIN to connect with the Support Line of the Division on our Left at I.26.a.0.0.

4. The Infantry Brigade in Divisional Reserve with one Machine Gun Company will be prepared -

   (a) to counter-attack to regain any part of the Outpost Line of Resistance which may be lost.

   (b) to counter-attack to regain any part of the 2nd Line which may be lost.

   (c) in case of emergency to occupy line from N.17.b. (connecting with the 2nd Line of 74th Div.) thence East of BLONDAIN - East of MARAIS - H.34.d. and b.
   The necessary reconnaissances will be made accordingly.

5. One Coy of 57th Bn. M.G.C. is affiliated to each of the Inf. Bdes. in the line.

These Companies are disposed in depth as far back as the 2nd line (inclusive)

A third Coy is in Support, with positions selected and routes reconnoitred to positions.

   4 guns on High Ground about O.13.a.7.9.

   4 " about O.8.b.7.8.

   4 " " N.30.d.9.3.

The fourth Coy is at Lt DARS earmarked for employment with the Reserve Infantry Brigade in the tasks enumerated in para. 4.

The necessary reconnaissances have been made.

          J. Workes LSH
           Capt. & Adjt.
          57th Bn. M.G.C.

29/10/18.

Distribution -
 "A" Coy
 "B" "
 "C" "
 "D" "
 S War Diary
  1 File.

App VII

SECRET.

57th BATTN. M.G.C.
ACTION IN EVENT OF ENEMY WITHDRAWAL.

1.   In the event of any weakening of the enemy's resistance, the following objectives are allotted to Brigades:-

RIGHT BRIGADE:

    1st Objective.   Line of Railway in O.16.b. - O.10.b. and O.4.c.

    2nd Objective.   LA TOMBE - Buildings in O.5.c.

    3rd Objective.   Ridge in P.8. and 9. and P.2.

LEFT BRIGADE.

    1st Objective.   Line of Railway in O.4.a. and I.3.3.

    2nd Objective.   KAIN-LA FOLIE.

    3rd Objective.   MT. ST. AUBERT which will be approached from the South in conjunction with advance of Right Bde. of the Division on our left, who will be advancing on LA TRINITE from the North.

2.   Having reached the above objectives, the 2 leading Brigades (each with 1 M.G.Coy & 2 Sections R.E.) under cover of advanced guards, will continue the advance. The Right Bde. will be directed on BECLERS and the Left Bde. on MELLES.
A proportion of R.E. and M.G's will accompany each advanced guard.
The approximate dividing line between Bdes. will be O.5. central - Q.1.central.

3. R.E.ARRANGEMENTS.

    Two footbridges have been constructed at I.32.central and I.26.c.7.5. respectively, and a barrel bridge at I.32.a.9.1. The destroyed iron bridge at I.32.a.7.3. can also be crossed by infantry.
The above will be available for the Infantry of the Left Brigade.
Two footbridges have been prepared and placed close to the river ready for putting across about O.3.d.3.3. These will be available for the right Brigade.
It is intended to construct heavy bridges for artillery and transport at O.10.c.95.30. O.3.d.35.35. I.32.a.8.3.
Estimated time of construction about 10 or 11 hours.

4.   The first bound forward of Bde. Report Centres will be FROYENNES for the Right Bde. and PONT-A-CHIN for the Left Bde.
After this the main cable route will be KAIN-BIZENCOURT- MOULIN - TRIEU de MELLES.
Brigades will establish their report centres and H.Q. on this line.
M.G.Coys will keep in close touch.

5.   Whenever enemy opposition checks the advance or when the limit of the advance for the day has been reached, arrangements will be made by each Bde. for protection for the night.

O.C.Coys will be responsible that a sufficient number of M.G's are in position to do this.

6.   The three support sections forward of WILLEMS will stand fast and await orders from their O.C.Coy who will act under orders of O.C. M.G.Bn.

7.   The Coy with Reserve Brigade in WILLEMS will act with its Brigade.

8.   Two platoons 2/5 L.N.L.R.(P) will be attached to each Coy moving forward with the advanced Brigades to assist in man handling guns and S.A.A. across the river.

They will report to O.C. forward Coys at Coy H.Q. as soon as the advance commences.

It is probable that it will be necessary to get guns across the river before the arrival of the carrying parties and in that case sections must carry forward guns with auxiliary mountings and as many belt boxes as possible leaving their Mk.IV tripods and the remainder of the S.A.A. to be brought on after them by the Pioneers.

29/10/18.

H.Oakeshott
Capt. & Adjt.
57th Battn.M.G.C.

A Coy
B "
C "
D "
2/War Diary.
1 File.

WAR DIARY
or
INTELLIGENCE SUMMARY.
(Erase heading not required.)

Army Form C. 2118.

57 Bn M.G.C.

Place	Date	Hour	Summary of Events and Information	Remarks and references to Appendices
	Nov. 1st		The Battalion began to move to Mons en Baroeul, staging at Chereng this night.	
	2nd		Move to Mons en Baroeul completed.	
	3rd		2nd Lieut. W.Archibald returned from II Corps Gas School. Casualties:- 140131 Pte.Elliott/S/M gassed	
	4th		Lieut. H.A.Oakeshott appointed adjutant vice Capt. T.N.F.Wilson and granted acting rank of Captain as from 28/9/18.	
			Lieut. E.R.Robinson appointed 2nd i/c "D" Coy. and granted acting rank of Captain while so employed as from 3/11/18.	
	5th		2nd Lieut. F.G.Voice returned from Rest Camp, Etaples.	
			"B" Coy. carried out firing on range at Fort Mons en Baroeul.	
			W.M. The King became Colonel in Chief of Machine Gun Corps.	
			A Recreation Room and Canteen opened at Ecole des Filles, Mons en Baroeul.	
	6th		2nd Lieut. J.A.Delaney admitted to hospital.	
			2nd Lieut. J.B.Taylor admitted to hospital.	
			No. 170727 Pte. Batten, E. awarded M.M. by Corps Commander.	
	7th		Riding School for officers started. In addition to ordinary training.	
			Court of Enquiry held to inquire into the loss of pads, surcingls, 37, and Buckets, water, 34; A new draft of 15 Reinforcements arrived from Base Depot.	
	8th		2nd Lieut. F.Emerson reported from Base and is taken on strength.	
	9th		"B" Coy. fired on range Fort Mons en Baroeul.	
			Capt. V.H.Wells and Lieut. J.M.Shepherd proceeded to G.H.Q.School, Camiers.	
	10th/12th		No Change.	
	13th		C.O. inspected all Coys. Lieut. E.Harris evacuated to hospital.	
	14th		G.O.C. 57th Div. inspected Battalion on Div. Playing Fields.	
			2nd Lieut. G.H.C.Turberville reported from Base Depot. 2nd Lieut. W.Young admitted to hospital.	
	15th		A draft of 22 reinforcements arrived from Base Depot.	
			Capt. H.A.Oakeshott proceeded on special leave to U.K.	
			"B" Coy. co-operated with 170 Bde. in a tactical scheme.	
	16th		Lieut. H.H.Ball proceeded on special leave to U.K. 2nd Lieut. J.F.Emerson proceeded to England for a tour of duty at M.G.T.C. Grantham.	
			16 animals sent to help locally farmers in ploughing. This was done daily.	
	17th		2nd Lieut. G.C.Tothill reported from leave to U.K.	

.... Lieut Col.
Commanding 57th Bgtn. M.G.C.

Army Form C. 2118.

WAR DIARY
or
INTELLIGENCE SUMMARY.
(Erase heading not required.)

Instructions regarding War Diaries and Intelligence Summaries are contained in F. S. Regs., Part II. and the Staff Manual respectively. Title pages will be prepared in manuscript.

Place	Date	Hour	Summary of Events and Information	Remarks and references to Appendices
	Nov. 18/20		No Change.	
	21st		2nd Lieut. J.Whiston reported from leave to U.K. A draft of 15 reinforcements arrived from Base Depot.	
	22nd		2nd Lieut. F.C.Voice proceeded on leave to U.K. 2nd Lieut. F.Houghton) Lieut. L.G.Pinnell) Reported from leave to U.K.	
	23rd		Lieut. R.W.Wilkinson reported from Base Depot.	
	24th		Lieut. J.B.Taylor evacuated to England sick. Draft of 4 drivers (reinforcements) reported from Advanced Horse Transport Depot.	
	25th		Maj. J. Robin was admitted to hospital.	
	26th		2nd Lieut. G.D.Green reported from V Army Infantry School.	
	27th		Lieut. J.M.Shepherd ceases to be Transport Officer of "C" Coy. as from 25/10/18.	
	28th		2nd Lieut. S.R.Hunt admitted to hospital. A draft of 18 reinforcements reported from Base Depot.	
	29th		Lieut. J. Whiston is appointed Section Officer in "B" Coy.	
	30th		Major. J. Robin died in hospital. Ploughing for local farmers ceased.	

............Lieut. Col.
Commanding 57th Battn M G C.

57 Bn for C.of S
Army Form C. 2118.
9/1/11

WAR DIARY
or
INTELLIGENCE SUMMARY

(Erase heading not required.)

Instructions regarding War Diaries and Intelligence Summaries are contained in F.S. Regs., Part II. and the Staff Manual respectively. Title pages will be prepared in manuscript.

Place	Date	Hour	Summary of Events and Information	Remarks and references to Appendices
	Dec. 1918.			
Mons en Baroeul (Lille).	1st.		Lieut. L.C.H.Chase to leave to Paris.	
	2nd.		Lieut. H.H.Ball & Lieut. L.F.M.Ackroyd from leave to U.K.	
			Lieut. J.M.Shephard from course at Camiers.	
	3rd.		2nd Lt. W.Archibald to leave U.K.	
	4th.		The Battalion marched from Mons to Carvin.	
Carvin. Gouves & Contenescourt.	6th.		The Battalion arrived at Gouves and went into billets and huts. "A" Coy. to Montenescourt.	
	8th.		Lieut. A.L.Thorne arrived from Base Depot. Posted to "D" Coy.	
			Lieut. A.Bedford arrived from Base Depot. Posted to "A" Coy.	
			Maj. N.S.St.G.Mansergh appointed 2nd in Command of Battalion.	
	10th.		Lieut. (A/Maj) W.Barber, M.C. proceeded to U.K. as draft conducting officer.	
			T/Capt.(A/Maj) K.S.Mason, M.C. reported from 58th Battn. M.G.C. and assumed command of "C" Coy.	
			21 coalminers despatched for demobilisation.	
	11th.		11 coalminers despatched for demobilisation.	
			Lieut. L.C.H.Chase returned from Paris.	
	12th.		Lieut. Cartwright to perform duties of B.T.O.	
	13th.		Capt. E.R.Robinson to U.K. on leave.	
			8 coalminers released.	
	14th.		2nd Lt. R.Riggs struck off strength whilst in U.K.	
			2nd Lt. W.W.Spendlove to U.K. draft-conducting.	
			Lieut. W.Monks returned to 57th Div. Sig. Coy. R.E. with 13 O.R. No. 5 Section.	
			12 coalminers released.	
	17th.		Parties to Cambrai by lorry to visit battlefield.	
	18th.		13 coalminers released.	
			1 coalminer released.	
	19th.		Maj. R.A.T.Miller to U.K. on one months leave.	
			Lieut. G.H.A.Hughes to 57th Div. H.Q. on duty.	
	20th.		2nd Lt. W.Archibald from leave.	
			Major G.L.O.Grundy to M.E.course, Audruicq.	
	21st		Capt. V.H.Wells to leave U.K.	
			2nd Lt. T.R.Binks and 33 O.R. to Arras as railway guard.	
			Salvage operations commenced.	

B. W. d. Puckle
Lieut. Col.
Commanding 57th Batn. M.G.C.

Army Form C. 2118.

WAR DIARY
or
INTELLIGENCE SUMMARY.
(Erase heading not required.)

Instructions regarding War Diaries and Intelligence Summaries are contained in F. S. Regs. Part II. and the Staff Manual respectively. Title pages will be prepared in manuscript.

Place	Date	Hour	Summary of Events and Information	Remarks and references to Appendices
OUVES.	Dec. 1918			
	22nd.		3 coalminers released.	
	23rd.		Capt. H.A.Oakeshott from leave and sick leave U.K.	
	24th.		Capt. S.Hall Patch relinquishes duties of Adjutant.	
	25th.		Capt. H.A.Oakeshott reassumes duties of Adjutant.	
	26th.		2nd Lt. A.J.Bedford and 27 O.R. to First Army Staging Camp.	
			30 O.R. to Cambrai by lorry to visit battlefield.	
			Lieut. G.H.A.Hughes returns from Div. H.Q.	
	27th.		7 O.R. released for demobilisation.	
	30th.		Lt.Col. B.H.Puckle, D.S.O. to leave U.K.	
			Major N.S.St.G.Mansergh assumes Command.	
	31st.		Lieut. F. Cartwright to Officers Rest House, Paris Plage.	
			2nd Lieut. H.E.T.Scowsill from U.K. leave.	
			2nd Lieut. F.C.Voice to First Army School of Farming, Etrun, as student.	
			Capt. C.H.Gadd to First Army School of Farming, Etrun, as instructor.	

REINFORCEMENTS.

12	O.R.	15/12/18.
42	O.R.	23/12/18.

CASUALTIES.

Accidentally Killed.

146923 Pte. Gobey, C.   1/12/18.

Died in Hospital.

116262 Pte. Maplethorpe, 2/12/18.
27108 "   Calvert, G. 5/12/18.

Evacuated sick and struck off strength.

42 O.R.

STRENGTH.

	Officers.	O.Rs.
1/12/18.	46.	885.
31/12/18.	49.	839.

B.H. Puckle, Lieut Col
Commanding 572nd Batn. M.G.C.

Army Form C. 2118.

WAR DIARY
or
INTELLIGENCE SUMMARY.
(Erase heading not required.)

Instructions regarding War Diaries and Intelligence Summaries are contained in F. S. Regs., Part II. and the Staff Manual respectively. Title pages will be prepared in manuscript.

57TH BATTALION MACHINE GUN CORPS

Place	Date	Hour	Summary of Events and Information	Remarks and references to Appendices
Sheet 51c Louvres Fontanescourt	1919 Jan 2		2/Lt. B. Archibald and 1u/Lt to XI Corps Co-ordination Camp. Capt. A. V. Ginaldaris from leave to U.K.	
	3		Lt. D. A. Shepherd and Lt. D. C. L. Chase to U.K. Lt. H. B. Barber, M.C. Then leave to U.K. Lt. H. R. Wilkinson to hospital. To o/r released for demobilization.	
	5		Battalion moved to Lapasco, Sett. H.Q. in Chateau. Lt. T. R. Ackerd from Course 286 Res. G. A. 2/Lt. J. H. C. Turberville from 286 Res. G. A. 3 o/r released for demobilization.	
Habarcq Sheet 51c	6		The undermentioned officers and men have been mentioned in the despatch of Field Marshal Sir Douglas Haig, K.T., G.C.B., G.C.V.O., K.C.I.E., Commander-in-Chief of the British Armies in France dated 8th November 1918, for distinguished and gallant service:- Maj. (O/L. Col.) J. .... Nelson, D.S.O., M.C., 57th Batt. M.G.C. Lieut. (A/Major) A.A. Hillier, M.C., 57th Batt. M.G.C. Lieut. L.A. Robinett 57th Batt. M.G.C. 30381 C.Q.M.S. Burr 57th Batt. M.G.C. 118443 Pte. M. Burton 57th Batt. M.G.C. 4 o/r relieved for demobilization.	
	9		Lt. H. H. Thomas from leave to U.K. 2/Lt. R. ....tarlund from course of Stokes Mortars, Halle, Wilts, to U.K. Lt. A. H. Thomas to Ret. of Station Permit. Lt. W. L. Ware to U.K. 14 line Lt. H. Beaton Leave to U.K. Major J. A. Beauclerqh M.C. to Lib...Trans School, Gidle Spadel, Ibbeault. Lt. J. R........head to B.H.Q. Observing duty.	
	10		3/4 o/r released for demobilization.	
	11		Capt. (A/Major) T. Smith, Groups—d to be 2nd in Command of Battalion. Lt. Acker to U.K. Duty Escorting duty. Lt. Col. F. H. Puello D.S.O. from Leave assumes command of Battalion.	
	12		49 o/r released for demobilization. 8 o/r released for demobilization.	

B. Aul Siebel
Lieut Col
Commanding 57th Battn M.G.C.

Army Form C. 2118.

WAR DIARY
or
INTELLIGENCE SUMMARY.
(Erase heading not required.)

Instructions regarding War Diaries and Intelligence Summaries are contained in F. S. Regs., Part II and the Staff Manual respectively. Title pages will be prepared in manuscript.

Place	Date	Hour	Summary of Events and Information	Remarks and references to Appendices
Habarcq	Jan 13		Capt. C. H. Gadd from 1st. Army School of Farming.	
	11		3/r released for demobilization.	
			C/Lt. H. T. Scowcroft to U K Draft conducting duty.	
	12		Lt. A. Wilkinson evacuated sick to U.K.	
	13		Capt. C. H. Gadd to U K Draft conducting duty.	
			Lt. P. Cartwright do do	
			Lt. G. C. Tothill do do	
	14		2/Lt. A. Reid to D.V.T. Salvage Cor.	
			2/Lt. W. Archibald taken on Pd. establishment of 21 Corps Concentration Camp.	
			2/Lt. S. D. Green to leave to U.K.	
	15		22/r released for demobilization.	
			Lt. A. S. Cecle to U K Draft conducting duty.	
	17		Capt. & V. V. Wells given leave to U.K.	
			Capt. N. E. St. C. Mansergh assumed command of "A" Company.	
	18		10 o/r released for demobilization.	
			Lt. G. H. A. Hughes to U K Draft conducting duty.	
	19		Major H. S. Mason M.C. assumed duty as 2nd. in command of Battalion.	
			10 o/r released for demobilization.	
			Battalion divided into groups as follows owing to reduction in numbers:-	
			No. 1 Group Capt. G. V. Cox M.C. "A")	
			No. 2 Group Major J. F. Robinson "C") B.H.Q.	
	20		4 o/r released for demobilization.	
			Major E. A. T. Mills arrived from U.K. to U.K. and assumed command of "B" Company.	
			Capt. V. V. Wells ceased to perform duties of O.C. "B" Company.	
			18 o/r released for demobilization.	
	21		Major J. F. Robinson assumed command of No. 1 Group.	
			Major E. A. T. Mills assumed command of No. 2 Group.	
			New Year Honours Gazette January 1st. 1919.	
	23		Lt. F. C. Voice from 1st. Army School of Farming.	
	25		Cent to U K Draft conducting duty.	
			Distinguished Conduct Medal 81541 C.S.M. Godwin M.J.	
			Meritorious Service Medal 68299 C.S.M. (Med.) 51238 C.Q.M.S. Crouch 29592 Sgt. W. 75.	

B. Dela Puebla Lieut Col.
Commanding 57th Bttn M.C.G.

Army Form C. 2118.

WAR DIARY
or
INTELLIGENCE SUMMARY.
(Erase heading not required.)

Instructions regarding War Diaries and Intelligence Summaries are contained in F. S. Regs., Part II. and the Staff Manual respectively. Title pages will be prepared in manuscript.

Place	Date	Hour	Summary of Events and Information	Remarks and references to Appendices
Habareq	Jan 27		Major L.C.Eason, C. to Officers Rest Camp, Paris Plage	
	28		Capt J.A.P.Hall-Patch to leave to U.K.	
	29		Lt. A.Shepherd from leave to U.K.	
	30		Lt. H.Robinson to leave to U.K.	
			2/Lt. J.Cowley to Arras Railhead vice 2/Lt. L.M.Blake returned.	
			Capt. A.V. Rissmiming (R.A.M.C.) to Divl. Sanitary Section for duty.	
	31		Lt. E.N.Pinnell to D K Draft conducting duty.	
			6 o/r relieved for demobilisation.	
			Reinforcements Decrease Strength Off o/r	
			46 o/r 71 o/r 1/1/19 69 839	
			31/1/19 43 748	

B. Hall Puebb ....Lieut Col
Commanding 57th Battn M.G.C.

WAR DIARY or INTELLIGENCE SUMMARY

Army Form C.2118.

57 Bn M.G Corps

Place	Date	Hour	Summary of Events and Information	Remarks and references to Appendices
Habarcq Chateau. Sheet 51Q	Feb. 2		2 O.Rs. released for demobilization. 2nd Lieut. F. Reynolds returned from First Army Infantry School.	
	3		5 O.Rs. released for demobilization.	
	4		2nd Lieut. S.R. Hunt reported from M.G. Base and taken on strength. Lieut. P. Cartwright, Lieut. G.C. Tothill, Lieut. F.G. Neale, 2nd Lieut. H.E.T. Scowsill 2nd Lieut. W.W. Spandlove retained for demobilization whilst on leave to U.K. and struck off strength.	
	6		10 O.Rs. released for demobilization.	
	7		3 O.Rs released for demobilization. Capt. J.S.P.Hall-Patch ceased to be employed as second-in-command Company 22-1-19 and is appointed Adjutant. Capt. H.A.Oakeshott ceased to be employed as Adjutant 22-1-19 and is second-in-command Company 23-1-19. Major G.L.O.Grundy attached to C.M.E.Depot and struck off strength. 2nd Lieut. M.J.Gouley from duty at ARRAS Railhead.	
	10		Allen, C.P. attached to Battalion.	
	11	Rev.B.	5 O.Rs. released for demobilization.	
	12		Lieut. L.M.F.Ackroyd demobilized whilst on draft-conducting duty and struck off strength. Major K.C.Mason, M.C. returned from Officers Rest House, PARIS PLAGE.	
	13		2 O.Rs. released for demobilization.	
	14		4 O.Rs. released for demobilization.	
	15		Lieut. H.S.Gent returned from leave to U.K. 2nd Lieut. F. Reynolds to leave to U.K. Major E.R.Robinson returned from leave to U.K. Lieut. L.G.Pinnell demobilized whilst on draft conducting duty and struck off strength as from 5-2-19.	
	16		Capt. J.J.S.P.Hall-Patch returned from leave to U.K.	
	18		Major K.S.Mason, M.C. to leave to U.K. Lieut. J. Whiston to leave to U.K. Lieut. M.J.Gouley to U.K. for demobilization. 2nd Lieut. S.R.Hunt to St Pol Railhead for duty.	
	21		Major E.R.Robinson ceased to command No.1.Group and assumed command of No.2.Group. Capt. G.V.Cox M.C. assumed command of No.1.Group.	

Army Form C. 2118.

WAR DIARY
OR
INTELLIGENCE SUMMARY
(Erase heading not required.)

Instructions regarding War Diaries and Intelligence Summaries are contained in F. S. Regs., Part II. and the Staff Manual respectively. Title pages will be prepared in manuscript.

Place	Date	Hour	Summary of Events and Information	Remarks and references to Appendices
Haberoq Chateau. Sheet 51º	Feb. 21		Capt. V.H.Wells retained at M.G.T.C. and struck off strength 28-1-19.	
	22		Lieut. A.L.Thorne from duty at St Pol Railhead.	
	23		Major R.A.T.Miller to U.K. for two months leave prior to reporting to M.G.T.C. and struck off strength.	
	24		Lieut. A.L.Thorne to U.K. for demobilization.	
	25		10 O.Rs. transferred to First Army Animal Staging Camp and struck off strength.	
			2nd Lieut. A.A.Reid to War Office on duty and struck off strength.	
			2nd Lieut. T.R.Binks to leave U.K.	
	26		Lieut. F.I.Taylor to leave (France).	
	28.		2nd Lieut. L.G.Naylor and Lieut. J.H.P.Jones to U.K. on draft conducting duty.	

Strength 1/3/19

Officers   O/r
   33   491

.... Lieut.Col.
Commanding 57th Battn. M.G.C.

Army Form C. 2118.

WAR DIARY
or
INTELLIGENCE SUMMARY.
(Erase heading not required.)

Instructions regarding War Diaries and Intelligence Summaries are contained in F.S. Regs., Part II and the Staff Manual respectively. Title pages will be prepared in manuscript.

Place	Date	Hour	Summary of Events and Information	Remarks and references to Appendices
Labarcq Chateau.	2/2/19		Lieut. V.C. Hanlyn to leave to Paris. M.R. released for demobilisation	
	3		Capt. G.V. Cox MC to leave to U.K.	
Met. 1–18	7		2nd Lieut. W. Young joined to 7AA Coy nth Garrison Bn R.F. and struck off	
Marœuil			Lieut. Y.C. Taylor from leave to Lille	
19 – 31	8		2nd Lieut. Y Reynolds from leave to U.K.	
Sheet 51c	10		2nd Lieut. Y Reynolds to St Pol Railhead for duty	
	11		2nd Lieut. M.J. Gouly to U.K. for demobilisation	
			2nd Lieut. S.R. Guest from duty at St Pol Railhead	
			2nd Lieut. J.A. Hanlyn from leave to Paris	
	14		2nd Lieut. Y.P. Birds from leave to U.K.	
			Lieut. H.W. Thirwell MC to leave to U.K.	
	15		25 O.R's released for demobilisation	
			2nd Lieut. C.E.C. Turberville struck off strength	
	17		Major H.S. Mason MC from leave to U.K.	
			Concert given by 1/5th Batta. Loyal North Lancs. Regt.	
	18		Battalion moved to Marœuil (Concentration Area)	O.O.2046.

Army Form C. 2118.

WAR DIARY
or
INTELLIGENCE SUMMARY.
(Erase heading not required.)

Instructions regarding War Diaries and Intelligence Summaries are contained in F.S. Regs., Part II. and the Staff Manual respectively. Title pages will be prepared in manuscript.

Place	Date	Hour	Summary of Events and Information	Remarks and references to Appendices
Habarcq Château.	Feb 19/19		Lieut Y Whales and 2nd Lieut Y R Birks transferred to 200th Bn M.G.C.	
Feb 1-18			100 O.R's transferred to 200th Bn M.G.C.	
Wacquil	20		2nd Lieut G.L. Naylor from leave to U.K.	
19 – 31	21		Lieut E.W. Bates M.C. to Hospital	
Sheet 51.E			220 O.R's transferred to 200th Bn M.G.C. 43 O.R's transferred to VI Corps Concentration Camp	
	23		Lieut E.G. Barker M.C., Lt. G.O. Green, Lt. J.A. Kerslyn, Lt. H.L. Gore transferred to 30th Bn M.G.C.	
			Lieut G.L. bon M.C., Lt. K.W. Showell M.C., Lt M. Shepherd, 2nd Lt G.L. Naylor transferred to 200th Bn MGC	
	25		2nd Lieut J.V. Hunt transferred to VI Corps Concentration Camp	
	26		48 O.R's transferred to 200 th Bn M.G.C.	
	27		Lieut Y Reynolds and 14 O.R's rejoined the Battalion from St Pol Railhead.	
	28		Lt. Col. B.H. Buckle D.S.O. transferred to 34th Bn M.G.C. as Second in Command	
			Major X. J. Macan M.C. assumed command of the Battalion	

Major.
Commanding 59th Bn. M.G.C.

SECRET.
Copy No. 4
Map Ref:- Sheet Sls. 1:40000
Date. 15- -19.

57th. Battn. Machine Gun Corps Operation Order No.46.

1. **INFORMATION.**
   The Battalion less animals will move to Concentration Area on March 18th. 1919 and encamp at L.3. A.6.7.

2. **DISPOSITIONS.**
   The head of the Battalion will pass starting point at M.8. d.5.6. at a time to be notified later.

3. **ORDER OF MARCH.**
   No.1 Group.   No.2.Group.

4. **DRESS.**
   Full marching order.

5. **B.H.Q.**
   B.H.Q. will close at MABAUGE at 12.00 hours 18th. March and open at MAROUIL on arrival.

6. **ADMINISTRATIVE.**
   Blankets will be loaded into limbers by groups by 09.00 hours 18th. inst.
   O.C. Groups will make their own arrangements for the transfer to the new camp of all beds and stoves that they require.
   On arrival O.C. Groups will arrange to accomodate their respective "drafts" in adjoining huts as a separate section.
   O.C. No.1.Group will detail 1 N.C.O. and 1 man and O.C. No.2.Group 2 men from the Cadre Establishment as a guard. This guard will mount at MAROUIL at 09.00 hours 17th. March, and will take 48 hours rations with them.
   O.C. Groups will render to this office by mid-day 16th. a return showing the number of electric lamps required by them, and the situation in which they desire them placed.

7. **TRANSPORT.**
   Separate orders have been issued to B.T.O.

8. **ADVANCE PARTIES.**
   O.C. Groups will detail one officer and 1.N.C.O. to meet the Adjutant at the new camp at 14.30 hrs 17th.inst.

9. **BILLETING CERTIFICATES.**
   All Billeting Certificates must be completed before leaving the present area. Clearance certificates on the usual Bn. pro forma will be rendered for all civilian billets occupied

10. **CLEANLINESS.**
    O.C. Groups will personally inspect all billets of their commands and render the usual cleanliness certificates to this office.

Groups will acknowledge.

Issued at 16.00 hours.

DISTRIBUTION.
1. H.Q. 57th. Division.
2. O.C. No.1.Group.
3. O.C. No.2. Group.
4. Q.M.
5. B.T.O.
6. File.   7/8. War Diary.

TRANSPORT ORDER (copy)
In connection with Battalion Operation Order No.48.

R.T.O. will arrange to move all packed limbers, 3 water carts and field cookers to the new area on 17th. inst., and will see that the guard detailed in above order is mounted on the waggon park.

He will move Battalion Stores and canteen, at times to be arranged by Q.M. and P.R.I. respectively.

Orderly Room Stores, C.O. and Adjutants kits will be loaded into G.S. Waggon by 14.00 hours 18th. inst.

B... mess kit will be packed into mess cart after mid-day meal on 18th. Inst.

All available benches chairs and tables will be moved to new area.

After completion of move all animals except 4 "H" draft horses will return to stables at MAROGUE. Sufficient personnel to attend to them will be left. Lieut. F.Houghton will be in charge of this party, which will remain at MAROGUE until the animals are evacuated. All harness and gear except nose bags, rugs, blankets, and stable head collar will be left at MAROGUE camp.

Captain Adjutant,
17TH Batn. M.G.C.

57th Batt. M.G.C.

WAR DIARY
INTELLIGENCE SUMMARY
(Erase heading not required.)

Army Form C. 2118.

57TH BATTALION, MACHINE GUN CORPS.

Place	Date	Hour	Summary of Events and Information	Remarks and references to Appendices
MARŒUIL Sheet 51c France	1919 April 4th		Major E.R. Robinson, Capt. H.O. Cubitt, Lt. A.E. Taylor, Lt. Houghton proceeded on demobilization UK for	
	" 4		1 O.R. proceeded to U.K. for demobilization	
	" 5		Lt. L. Reynolds transferred to 200th Bn M.G.C.	
	" 5		31 O.R. transferred to 200th Batt M.G.C.	
	" 7		H.Q.R.	
	" 8		Lieut. F.C. Vozer proceeded to U.K. on special leave	
	" 9		15 O.R's transferred to 200th Bn M.G.C	
	" 9		2nd Lieut J.R. Hunt returned from leave to U.K.	
	" 10		2nd Lieut E. Donaldson 9th & 2nd Lt. R. returned to the Unit	
			Lieut H.S. Cant proceeded to 200th Batt. M.G.C	
	" 12		Lieut. W.H. Bull proceeded to U.K. on special leave	
	" 18		Lieut. K.R. Ball & Lieut. F.C. Vozer reported from leave to U.K.	
	" 22		2 O.R's transferred to 200th Bn M.G.C.	
	" 28		Lieut. W.H. Bull proceeded on leave to U.K. on return	

Major.
Commanding 57th Batt. M.G.C.

WAR DIARY
INTELLIGENCE SUMMARY.

(Erase heading not required.)

Army Form C. 2118.

51 Bn M G Coy

Place	Date	Hour	Summary of Events and Information	Remarks and references to Appendices
MAROEUIL Sheet 51c France.	1919 May 6		14 O.Rs transferred to 200th Battn. M.G.C.	
	9		1 O.R. do	
			Lieut. H. H. Ball returned from leave to U.K.	
	11		A & B Coys entrained at MAROEUIL Station for HAVRE	
			Lieut. L. G. Voice admitted 12th Stationary Hospital ST POL	
	13.		1. O.R. Strength Increase.	
	14		4. O.Rs Transferred to 200th Battn. M.G.C.	
	18		A & B Coys embarked at HAVRE on S.S. "WARFARE". 2nd Lt. S.R Hunt O.C. Cadres.	
	19		do disembarked at SOUTHAMPTON.	
	20		Capt. J.S. Hall-Patch proceeded on leave to U.K.	
	24		4 O.Rs " " " "	
	25		3 " " " "	
	26		10 " proceeded on leave to U.K.	

www.ingramcontent.com/pod-product-compliance
Lightning Source LLC
Chambersburg PA
CBHW081435160426
43193CB00013B/2287